C000180855

THE VILLA PARK
ENCYCLOPEDIA
An A-Z of Aston Villa FC

Titles available in this series

The Anfield Encyclopedia: an A–Z of Liverpool FC
The Old Trafford Encyclopedia: an A–Z of Manchester United FC
The Highbury an A–Z of Arsenal FC
The Elland Road Encyclopedia: an A–Z of Leeds United FC
The Stamford Bridge Encyclopedia: an A–Z of Chelsea FC
The Maine Road Encyclopedia: an A–Z of Manchester City FC
The White Hart Lane Encyclopedia: an A–Z of Tottenham Hotspur FC
The St James's Park Encyclopedia: an A–Z of Newcastle United FC
The Hawthorns Encyclopedia: an A–Z of West Bromwich Albion FC
The Hillsborough Encyclopedia: an A–Z of Sheffield Wednesday FC
The Villa Park Encyclopedia: an A–Z of Aston Villa FC

THE VILLA PARK ENCYCLOPEDIA

An A-Z of Aston Villa FC

Dean Hayes

MAINSTREAM
PUBLISHING

EDINBURGH AND LONDON

Copyright © Dean Hayes, 1997

All rights reserved

The moral right of the author has been asserted

First published in Great Britain in 1997 by
MAINSTREAM PUBLISHING COMPANY (EDINBURGH) LTD
7 Albany Street
Edinburgh EH1 3UG

ISBN 1 85158 959 7

No part of this book may be reproduced or transmitted in any form or by any means without written permission from the publisher, except by a reviewer who wishes to quote brief passages in connection with a review written for insertion in a magazine, newspaper or broadcast

A catalogue record for this book is available from the British Library

Typeset in Janson
Printed and bound in Great Britain by The Cromwell Press, Melksham

DEDICATION

For Aston Villa fans everywhere!

ACKNOWLEDGEMENTS

The author wishes to thank Aston Villa FC and the Association of Statisticians for their help in producing this book, and all at Mainstream Publishing for their support in producing books in this series.

PHOTOGRAPHS

The photographs in this book have been supplied by the *Lancashire Evening Post*, Les Gold Promotions and from the author's personal collection. All cigarette cards are reproduced from the collection of Peter Stafford.

ABANDONED MATCHES. A match may be called off by the referee whilst it is in progress when conditions do not permit it to be completed. Far fewer matches are abandoned than used to be the case, because if there is some doubt about playing the full game, the match is likely to be postponed. Villa travelled to Olive Grove to play Sheffield Wednesday on 26 November 1898 and were losing 3–1 with just 11½ minutes to play when the match was abandoned. The referee had been late in getting to the ground and so it was too dark to complete the game. The Football League made Villa travel back to Sheffield on 13 March 1899 to play the remaining minutes. Bedingfield, who scored in the first game, did not play the remaining 11½ minutes, his place going to Billy Garraty, but to no avail; Wednesday scored again to make it 4–1. A friendly between Glasgow Rangers and Aston Villa at Ibrox on 9 October 1976 was abandoned after fans threw bottles onto the pitch and fought with police.

AGGREGATE SCORE. Villa's highest aggregate score in any competition came in the Football League Cup competition of 1985–86. Playing Exeter City, Villa notched up 12 goals over the two legs. They won the first leg at St James's Park 4–1, with all the goals scored by Simon Stainrod, and then 8–1 at Villa Park.

AITKEN, CHARLIE. One of the club's all-time greats, Charlie Aitken holds the club record for the most league appearances with 561. Born in Edinburgh, he made his Villa debut in the final game of the 1960–61 season in a 4–1 win over Sheffield Wednesday. The following season he made the left-back spot his own after Gordon Lee had switched to right-back and John Neal had lost his place. Aitken went from strength to strength and very rarely missed a game, being an ever-present in five seasons. During his first few seasons with the club, he won three Scotland Under-23 caps and a League Cup runners-up prize in 1963. In 1970, he was granted a testimonial against Coventry City and at the end of the season gained another runners-up award in the League Cup. The following season, he was an important member of the Villa side that won the third division championship and in December 1973 overtook Billy Walker's record for most league appearances. In 1974–75, one of Aitken's ever-present seasons, he won a League Cup winners' tankard and helped the club win promotion to the first division. Not surprisingly, he was named Midland Footballer of the Year. The popular Scot decided to leave Villa Park in the summer of 1976 to play for New York Cosmos in the NASL after playing in 659 first-team games and scoring 16 goals.

ALDIS, PETER. A former chocolate-maker with Cadburys, Peter Aldis made his Villa debut at left-back in a 2–1 defeat at Arsenal in March 1951. He played in the first 17 games of the 1951–52 season but was forced to miss the rest of the campaign after undergoing a cartilage operation. The following season, he scored the only goal of his Villa career, a spectacular 35-yard header in the 3–0 home win over Sunderland. He won an FA Cup winners' medal in 1957 and captained the club in 1958–59, his last season at Villa Park. He had given the club excellent service, playing in 294 league and Cup games before joining Hinckley Athletic in the summer of 1960. After helping Hinckley win the Southern League First Division title, he went to Australia as player-manager of Slavia, later playing for FC Wilhelmina and the Lions Club in the Victoria State League. He returned to England in the mid-1960s as manager of non-league Alvechurch.

ALLEN, ALBERT. Albert Allen marked his international debut for England with a hat-trick against Ireland in Belfast on 31 March

1888. A member of the Villa side that played Wolverhampton Wanderers in the club's first Football League game, Allen scored Villa's first league hat-trick in the 9–1 win over Notts County on 29 September 1888. He ended that season as the club's top scorer with 18 goals in 21 league appearances. In 1889–90 he scored another hat-trick as Villa beat Burnley 6–2 at Turf Moor, this time finishing the season as joint top scorer. Illness forced Allen's retirement at the age of just 24 and though he was able to work, he died in October 1899, aged 32.

ALLEN, JIMMY. A stylish centre-half, Jimmy Allen began his footballing career with Portsmouth and in 1934 won an FA Cup runners-up medal. At the end of that season, he joined Villa for what was then a record fee of £10,775. He had been capped twice by England during his time at Fratton Park and after making his Villa debut in the opening game of the 1934–35 season, soon settled into the side. Injury reduced the number of his appearances in 1936–37, but he was back to his best the following season, helping the club win promotion to the first division. Though he scored only three goals in his 160 league and Cup games for Villa before the outbreak of war, he did score one for Poole Town from fully 60 yards before he joined Portsmouth. During the hostilities, he guested for Birmingham City, Fulham and Portsmouth.

Jimmy Allen

ANDERSON, WILLIE. Liverpool-born winger Willie Anderson was understudy to George Best at Manchester United for four seasons and though in that time he appeared in only 12 first-team games, two were major Cup semi-finals. He was transferred to Aston Villa in January 1967 for a fee of £20,000, making his debut in a 3–1 defeat at Chelsea. An ever-present in seasons 1967–68 and 1970–71, his best season goalscoring-wise was 1971–72 when he scored 16 goals in 48 League and Cup matches. He won a League Cup runners-up medal in 1971 and a third division championship medal the following season. He joined Cardiff City in the summer of 1972 but after five seasons at Ninian Park went to play in the NASL.

APPEARANCES. Charlie Aitken holds the record for the most appearances in an Aston Villa shirt, with a total of 659 games to his credit between 1961 and 1976. In all, Aitken played in 561 league games, 35 FA Cup games, 61 Football League Cup games and two European matches.

ASTLEY, DAI. Though standing 6ft tall, this Welsh ex-miner weighed only 11st and looked far too frail to make the grade in league football. However, after impressing for Charlton Athletic in four seasons at the Valley, he signed for Aston Villa in the summer of 1931. Astley was a superb marksman and after scoring on his debut in a 3–0 win over Portsmouth, went on to score 100 goals for Villa in 173 league and Cup appearances. He scored six hat-tricks for the club, three of them coming in the 1934–35 season. He had won one Welsh cap in his time at Charlton and went on to win another nine while with Villa. He left Villa Park in November 1936 to play for Derby County, where

Dai Astley

he scored 29 goals in his first 30 games for the club. In January 1939 after scoring 49 goals in 98 appearances for the Rams, he was allowed to join Blackpool. He managed only six goals in 20 games for the Seasiders and after guesting for a number of clubs during the Second World War, he went to coach Inter Milan.

ASTON LOWER GROUNDS. The Aston Lower Grounds were situated directly opposite where Villa Park would later be built. A number of sporting activities took place there including athletics championships, cycle races and lacrosse games. W.G. Grace, the great Gloucestershire and England batsman, starred in an exhibition game against Australia; the men from down under beat an England XI inside four and a half hours. Two FA Cup semi-finals were played there in 1884 and 1886, and in 1887 Buffalo Bill Cody brought his famous Wild West Rodeo Show to the Lower Grounds. Villa played a number of games there during 1875–76. The visit of Wednesbury Old Athletic in April 1876 attracting a crowd of 2,000.

ASTON PARK. After their first-ever match at Wilson Road, Villa played on Aston Hall's old deer park, then called the Aston Upper Grounds (Aston Park today). The biggest crowd to attend a match there was 1,500 for the visit of St George's Excelsior in September 1875.

ATHERSMITH, CHARLIE. One of the game's fastest wingers, Charlie Athersmith spent the 1890s with Villa, scoring 85 goals in 308 league and Cup matches. He joined Villa from Unity Gas Depot FC, making his debut at home to Preston in May 1891, a month before John Devey was signed. Devey and Athersmith formed an outstanding right-wing partnership with Devey helping to make Athersmith into a supreme footballer. Athersmith was rewarded with two FA Cup winners' medals, five league championship winners' medals and 12 England caps, plus nine appearances for the Football League. In Villa's double season of 1896–97, he won every honour available, adding England caps against Scotland, Wales and Ireland to his double medals. The previous season he is reported to have played a whole match shielding from torrential rain under an umbrella given to him by a spectator. After leaving Villa Park in the summer of 1901, he played in over 100 games for Small Heath before becoming Grimsby Town's trainer in June 1907.

ATKINSON, DALIAN. After only occasional appearances for Ipswich Town, Dalian Atkinson became a first-team regular in February 1988. He scored eight goals in 13 full appearances to the end of the season, including a magnificent hat-trick against Middlesbrough. In June 1989 he joined Sheffield Wednesday and though he stayed for only 12 months, he became a great favourite with the Hillsborough crowd. Sold to Real Sociedad for £1.7 million, he scored 12 goals in 29 games before being re-signed in July 1991 by his former manager at Wednesday, Ron Atkinson, who had taken over at Villa Park. He scored on his debut for Villa in a 3–2 win at Sheffield Wednesday of all places. A succession of niggling injuries prevented him from playing in more games than he did for Villa. Yet some of his goals will remain etched in the memory, perhaps none more so than his 'Match of the Day – Goal of the Season' competition winner against Wimbledon in 1992–93. He scored one of the goals that defeated Manchester United in the 1994 League Cup final, but after scoring 34 goals in 106 league and Cup appearances, he left Villa for Fenerbahce.

ATKINSON, RON. Liverpool-born Ron Atkinson was brought up in the West Midlands. On leaving school, he worked as an apprentice engineer at the BSA tool factory. Rejected by Wolves, he signed for Villa in 1956, having been spotted playing as an inside-forward for BSA Tools. Unable to make the first team at Villa Park, he was given a free transfer and joined Headington United in 1959. They changed their name to Oxford United the following year and Atkinson, converted to wing-half, captained the side to great success. They won the

Ron Atkinson

Southern League championship in both the 1960–61 and 1961–62 seasons and replaced the defunct Accrington Stanley in the Football League. Atkinson served Oxford for 15 years, playing in 560 matches, 383 of them in the Football League. He helped them win promotion from the fourth division in 1965 and climb into the second division three years later. He began his managerial career at Kettering Town and, in his first season, took them to the Southern League North Division championship and promotion to the Premier League. He then joined Cambridge United and led them to the fourth division championship. They were already on course for a second successive promotion when he joined West Bromwich Albion. After Albion had finished third in the first division in 1979–80, Atkinson moved to Manchester United. He immediately went back to his former club to sign Bryan Robson for £1.5 million. United won the FA Cup in 1983 and 1985 but in

1986 Big Ron was sacked, receiving £100,000 in compensation. After a short second spell at the Hawthorns, he was enticed to join Atletico Madrid but, after just 96 days, he was sacked, despite taking the club to third position in the league. In February 1989, he became manager of Sheffield Wednesday and, despite suffering relegation in 1989–90, returned to the first division the following season and won the League Cup. However, in the summer of 1991, Atkinson turned his back on the Hillsborough club and joined Aston Villa. In 1992–93, the inaugural season of the Premier League, Atkinson took Villa to the runners-up spot but, though he spent heavily in the close season, Villa finished tenth in 1993–94. However, they won the League Cup, completely outplaying one of his former clubs, Manchester United. In October 1995, Villa's season began to fall apart and after a run of eight defeats and a draw in nine matches, he was dismissed just weeks after he had agreed an extension on his contract.

He took over at Coventry City before handing over the reins to his assistant, Gordon Strachan.

ATTENDANCE – AVERAGE. Villa's average home league attendances for the last ten seasons have been as follows:

1986–87	18,171	1991–92	24,814
1987–88	18,342	1992–93	29,594
1988–89	23,310	1993–94	29,015
1989–90	25,544	1994–95	29,756
1990–91	25,663	1995–96	32,616

ATTENDANCE – HIGHEST. The record attendance at Villa Park is 76,588 for the sixth round FA Cup game with Derby County on 2 March 1946. Villa lost 4–3. The record attendance for a Football League match gathered on 27 December 1949 when 69,492 watched Villa beat Wolverhampton Wanderers 5–1 with Welsh international Trevor Ford scoring four of the goals.

ATTENDANCE – LOWEST. The lowest attendance at Villa Park for a competitive game involving the club's first team came on 13 February 1915 when a crowd of just 2,900 saw Villa play out a goalless draw with Bradford City in a first division match.

AWAY MATCHES. Aston Villa's best away wins came in the FA Cup fourth-round replay at Clapton Orient on 30 January 1929 when they won 8–0, and at Leicester City on 2 January 1932 when they won 8–3 in a first division match. Villa's worst defeat away from home is the 8–1 thrashing handed out by Blackburn Rovers in the FA Cup competition of 1888–89. The highest scoring away match Villa were involved in came in 1927–28 when they went down 7–5 to Newcastle United.

AWAY SEASONS. The club's highest number of away wins came in 1987–88. They won 13 of their 22 matches and finished as runners-up to Millwall in division two. In 1975–76, Villa failed to win a single away game when finishing 16th in the first division.

B

BACHE, JOE. Joe Bache was an immensely talented inside-forward who spent 14 seasons with Aston Villa, scoring 185 goals in 473 first-team appearances. His first game for Villa was against the German club Berlin FC in 1901, though his first league game was at Notts County the following month. One of the club's greatest-ever forwards, he scored eight hat-tricks, his first coming on 7 November 1903 when he scored all three goals in Villa's 3–1 win over Newcastle United. Forming an outstanding left-wing partnership with Albert Hall, Bache eventually succeeded Howard Spencer as Villa's captain and went on to win two FA Cup winners' medals and a league championship medal during his time with the club. Capped seven times by England, he won his first against Wales in 1903 and his last against Scotland eight years later. He and Hall were England's left-wing pairing against Ireland at Belfast in 1910, thus carrying on the tradition first established by Devey and Athersmith in 1892. Bache appeared in four wartime matches, but in the summer of 1920, he left to become player-manager of Mid-Rhondda FC. He later coached Grimsby Town and the Rot Weiss club of Frankfurt before returning to Villa Park in 1927 as the club's second-team coach.

BAKER, ALAN. An England schoolboy and youth international, Alan Baker turned professional in 1961, making his debut at

Fulham in a 1–1 draw towards the end of the 1960–61 season. He served the club well over the next five seasons, playing in 109 league and Cup games and picking up a League Cup runners-up award when Villa lost over two legs to Birmingham City in 1963. He joined Walsall in the summer of 1966 and played in 150 games for the Fellowes Park club before leaving the game in 1972.

BALL, TOMMY. Born on Tyneside in February 1899, Tommy Ball was signed from Newcastle United on 17 January 1920 as Villa sought to strengthen their defence. A powerfully built centre-half, he was a great prospect and was being groomed to replace Frank Barson, who had revitalised an ailing Villa side. Ball made a disastrous start in an Aston Villa shirt. He played in the heart of the defence, as Villa went down 6–3 at home to Bolton Wanderers. In fact, his next game for Villa at the start of the following season saw them travel to Burnden Park, where this time they went down 5–0 to Bolton! After this, both Ball and the Villa defence settled down and he went on to make 77 league and Cup appearances before being shot dead by his policeman neighbour. He was only 24 years of age.

BARBER, TOMMY. Born within 100 yards of Newcastle United's St James's Park, Tommy Barber began his league career with Bolton Wanderers. In his first full season, he helped the Trotters win the second division championship and in 1911–12 was an ever-present. On Christmas Eve 1912, Aston Villa paid £1,950 for his services, the profits allowing the Wanderers to cover the Great Lever Stand on their Burnden Park ground. He made his debut at Bradford City four days later and went on to settle well into a Villa side that was heading for the 1913 FA Cup final. Clem Stephenson, Villa's inside-left had dreamed that Barber would head the game's winning goal against Sunderland and so it proved. Barber joined the Footballers' Battalion during the First World War and after the hostilities ended had spells with Stalybridge and Merthyr Tydfil before signing for Walsall in 1921. Sadly, he died at Nuneaton in September 1925 from tuberculosis at the age of 39.

BARRETT, EARL. After failing to make progress at Manchester City, where he was loaned out to Cardiff City, Earl Barrett was transferred to Oldham Athletic. In 1989–90 he moved from his usual full-back position to centre-back and was an ever-present as the Latics, losing League Cup finalists, progressed to the semi-finals of the FA Cup. He appeared in every match the following season too and hardly put a foot wrong as the club won the second division championship. He was then selected for the international tour of Australasia in the summer of 1991 and made his England debut against New Zealand. He joined Villa in February 1992 for £1.7 million and the following season was an ever-present, going from strength to strength. Rarely missing a game, Barrett had made 143 league and Cup appearances when he was transferred to Everton in January 1995 for the same fee he had cost Villa.

BARSON, FRANK. Born at Grimesthorpe, near Sheffield, Frank Barson was a blacksmith before becoming a professional footballer. His first club, Barnsley, had a reputation for developing hard players in those days and centre-half Barson was no exception. Following a disagreement with the Barnsley board, he was allowed to leave Oakwell and in October 1919 Villa paid £2,850 for his services. He was a member of the Villa side that won the FA Cup the following year, a year in which he also won his only England cap. Wales won 2–1 at Highbury to record their first victory on English soil. Barson was a controversial character, serving probably more suspensions than any other English player. He was once rumoured to have pulled a gun on the Villa manager! However, Manchester United ignored these rumours and in the summer of 1922 paid Villa £5,000 for the fierce-tackling centre-half. He was highly respected at Old Trafford, playing in 152 league and Cup games in six years and helping the Reds into the first division. United gave him a free transfer in 1928. He signed for Watford and subsequently played for Hartlepool United, Wigan Borough, was player-manager of Rhyl and manager of Stourbridge. He returned to Villa Park to coach in 1935 but after the Second World War, he became trainer to Swansea Town before taking up a similar position with Lye Town.

BARTON, TONY. An aggressive outside-right, Tony Barton began his professional career with Fulham in 1954, before playing for Nottingham Forest, where he never really settled, and Portsmouth. At Fratton Park, he was in the same side as Ron

Saunders and provided many of the crosses which Saunders converted into goals as Pompey won the third division title in 1961–62. He stayed with Portsmouth after retiring from the playing side as first-team coach before joining Saunders at Villa Park as his assistant. He was promoted to team manager in February 1982 after Saunders left and guided Villa to a European Cup final victory four months later. He lost his job at Villa Park at the end of the 1983–84 season and joined Northampton Town, but suffered a heart attack a year later and was forced to leave. Happily, he recovered and joined Chris Nicholl at Southampton.

BERESFORD, JOE. One of the most popular players to pull on a Villa shirt, Joe Beresford joined the club from Mansfield Town in 1927. Playing at inside- or centre-forward, the stocky Beresford possessed a powerful shot and in only his second game for the club hit a hat-trick in a 7–2 win over Portsmouth. When Villa scored a record-breaking 128 goals in 1930–31, Beresford scored 14 of them, including another hat-trick, this time against Leicester City. His form during the early 1930s was such that he won an England cap against Czechoslovakia in 1934, yet when Villa's first-ever manager Jimmy McMullan arrived, Beresford was allowed to leave. He had scored 73 goals in 251 league and Cup games. He joined Preston North End and appeared in the Deepdale club's FA Cup final side of 1937 in the match against Sunderland.

CARRERAS CIGARETTES

J. BERESFORD
ASTON VILLA (1ST DIV.)

Joe Beresford

BEST STARTS. Aston Villa were unbeaten for the first 11 games of the 1932–33 season. They won eight and drew three of these matches before losing 3–1 at West Bromwich Albion on 29 October 1932. They finished runners-up to Arsenal in the first division.

18

BIRCH, PAUL. A member of the Aston Villa FA Youth Cup winning side of 1980, Paul Birch made his first-team debut in the 1–0 win at home to Sunderland on 29 August 1983. Over the next ten seasons, the popular right-sided midfield man scored 24 goals in 212 league and Cup appearances for the Villans before joining Wolverhampton Wanderers for £400,000 in February 1991. Despite suffering a number of injuries at Molineux, he appeared in 165 first-team games before joining Preston North End on loan in March 1996.

Paul Birch

BLACKBURN, GEORGE. Signed by Villa as an amateur from Hampstead Town, a local youth side, George Blackburn turned professional in 1921 and made his debut at Bradford City in March of that year. A hard-working left-half, he played in 145 first- team games for Villa over a period of six years, picking up an FA Cup final losers' medal in 1924, the season he played for England against France. He moved on to Cardiff City, spending five years at Ninian Park before joining Mansfield Town. With the Bluebirds he won two Welsh Cup winners' medals and a runners-up medal in the same competition. In 1937 he became trainer at Birmingham City, leaving in 1946 after the Blues had won the Football League (South) championship.

BLAIR, DANNY. Born just a stone's throw from Celtic's Parkhead Stadium, Danny Blair studied agriculture and farming in Ireland and Canada and played his early football in those countries. At the age of 18, he returned to Scotland and signed for Clyde. Though he was on the small side, standing just 5ft 6½ ins and wearing size five boots, his appearance was deceptive. In his six years at Firhill Park he won seven full caps for Scotland. He joined Villa in November 1931 for a fee of £7,500, making his debut in a 5–1 win over Blackpool. However, in the next game Villa lost 3–0 at the Hawthorns and Blair was blamed by many fans for the defeat. A player with good positional sense, he worked hard at his game and soon won over his critics. He won another Scottish cap, playing against Wales in 1933. The strong-tackling full-back played in 138 first-team games for Villa before being allowed to join Blackpool in the summer of 1936. He played in 126 games for the Seasiders, later becoming coach at Bloomfield Road.

BLANCHFLOWER, DANNY. One of the greatest attacking wing-halves of all-time, Danny Blanchflower began his professional career with Glentoran. In 1947, he played for the Irish League against the Football League at Goodison Park and impressed many people; this led to a move to Barnsley in April 1949 for a fee of £6,500. Just six months later, he made his international debut for Northern Ireland against Scotland at Windsor Park, but was on the losing side as the Scots won 8–2. In March 1951, he moved to Aston Villa for £15,000 and made his debut on St Patrick's Day in a 3–2 victory over Burnley. As at Barnsley, his intellectual approach to the game and his passion for trying new ideas met with resistance and in December 1954, after appearing in 155 league and Cup games for Villa, he joined Spurs for a fee of £30,000. He was made captain at White Hart Lane and also took Northern Ireland into the 1958 World Cup finals where they reached the quarter-finals having beaten Czechoslovakia 3–2 with a team badly hit by injuries. He captained the side to the league and Cup double in 1960–61, the first time it had been achieved this century. He also scored from a penalty in the Cup final victory over Burnley the following year. He was voted Footballer of the Year in both 1958 and 1961. Altogether he played in 56 internationals for the Irish, including 41 consecutively. When he retired from the game, he started a career as a journalist writing for the *Sunday Express*. Blanchflower made a brief excursion into football management in December 1978 when he took charge of Chelsea but resigned after nine months.

BOSNICH, MARK. Australian Mark Bosnich joined Manchester United as a 17-year-old non-contract player from Sydney Croatia and made three appearances in two years at Old Trafford. The Reds were hoping to sign him but problems in obtaining a work permit forced him to return home to Australia in August 1991. It came completely out of the blue when Villa announced his signing in February 1992, the work permit problem having been resolved.

Despite making an impressive debut at Luton in April that year, he began the following campaign in the reserves as Nigel Spink's deputy. His next first-team opportunity arrived in February 1993 when Spink was injured. Since then, the Australian international has not looked back; he has been the club's regular number one. He was ever present in 1995–96 and collected his second League Cup winners' medal in three years. A brave goalkeeper, one of the best in the Premier League, he has now appeared in well over 150 first-team games for the club.

BOWEN, TEDDY. Born at Hednesford, Teddy Bowen signed professional forms for Villa in January 1924 and made his debut in a 2–0 win at Cardiff City. Initially, he struggled to become a regular due to the form of Mort and Smart, but in 1926–27 he did break through and for the next five seasons he turned in some outstanding performances. A dedicated professional, he lost his place after Villa signed Blair and Nibloe for the full-back positions and in October 1934 after appearing in 199 first-team games for Villa, he joined Norwich City. He was an ever-present in his first season at Carrow Road, Norwich's first in the second division, and went on to play in over 130 games for the Canaries. After the Second World War, he returned to his birthplace to work for the Hednesford and District Social Services Department.

BOXING. Villa Park has staged a number of British championship boxing contests, including the 1948 promotion when Dick Turpin became the first black boxer to win a British title. Another well-known fighter to appear at Villa Park was the Midlands based Irishman Danny McAlinden.

BRADLEY, KEITH. After signing professional forms for Villa in May 1963, Keith Bradley had to wait until February 1965 before making his league debut in the local derby at St Andrews, when Villa beat Birmingham City 1–0. He did not make the right-back position his own until the 1966–67 season, then had to fight for his place with Mick Wright until 1970–71 when he again became first choice. That season he won a League Cup runners-up medal when Villa went down 2–0 to Tottenham Hotspur. He scored only two goals for Villa, both in the space of ten days in the 1966–67 season, bringing victories over the north-east clubs, Newcastle United and Sunderland. In 1971–72, he gained a third division championship medal but in November 1972, after spending a month on loan with Peterborough United, he joined the London Road club on a permanent basis.

BRAWN, BILLY. After playing his early football with his home town club, Wellingborough Town, Billy Brawn played for Northampton Town and Sheffield United before signing for Villa in December 1901. He made his debut for the club the following month at Blackburn Rovers, but was injured and did not play again until 1902–03. At 6ft 1in and 13st 5lbs, he was tall and heavy for a winger, but he won two England caps in 1904 and an FA Cup winners' medal in 1905, before leaving Villa Park the following year to play for Middlesbrough. He later played for Chelsea and Brentford, where he subsequently became a director.

BREMNER, DES. Beginning his professional career at Easter Road, midfielder Des Bremner played in 255 first-team matches for Hibernian before joining Villa for £250,000 in September 1979 with Joe Ward going in the opposite direction. Whilst with Hibernian, he represented the Scottish League, won nine Under-23 caps and in 1976 won his only Scottish cap, coming on as substitute for Kenny Dalglish in the match against Switzerland. He also gained runners-up medals in the Scottish League Cup final of 1975 and the

Des Bremner

Scottish Cup final of 1979. After making his Villa debut in a goalless draw against Arsenal, he went on to appear in 107 consecutive league games before he was injured in a 3–1 win over Wolves in March 1982. During that run, Villa won the league championship and with Bremner's tireless play a great feature of their game, went on to win the European Cup and European Super Cup. In October 1984, after appearing in 226 first-team games, he moved to Birmingham City, helping the Blues win promotion to the first division. He later played for Fulham and Walsall before ending his career with Stafford Rangers.

BROOME, FRANK. Frank Broome was playing for Berkhamsted Town in the Spartan League when Aston Villa gave him a trial in a Colts match during which he scored six goals! Although rather frail and on the small side, he had great speed and good positional sense and the club had no hesitation in signing him. He made his first-team debut at Portsmouth towards the end of the 1934–35 season, ending the campaign with three goals from seven matches. The following season, Villa were relegated and Broome was restricted to 16 appearances that brought him 11 goals. In 1936–37, he scored 28 goals in 38 league appearances but for the next campaign, manager Jimmy Hogan switched Broome to

Frank Broome

outside-right. Using his electrifying pace, Broome's powerful shooting brought him 20 goals as Villa won the second division championship. During his time at Villa Park, he won seven England caps. His first international appearance was against Germany in the infamous Berlin match when the England players, on the instructions of the Foreign Office, were forced to give a Nazi salute. After playing in the opening game of the 1946–47 season, he was transferred to Derby County where he scored 45 goals in 119 outings. In 1949, he joined Notts County, helping them win the third division (South) championship in his first season. He later played for Brentford before ending his Football

League days at Crewe. He wound up his playing career with Shelbourne in the League of Ireland. After a spell as reserve team coach and caretaker manager at Notts County, he managed Exeter City and Southend United before emigrating to Australia to be involved in the game down under. Six years later he rejoined Exeter as manager until taking up a coaching post in the Middle East.

BROTHERS. There have been a number of instances of brothers playing for Aston Villa. Arthur 'Digger' Brown who scored four goals on his international debut for England, appeared in 22 of Villa's first 25 FA Cup ties before ill-health forced him to retire from the game. His place in the side was taken by his younger brother Albert who scored 55 goals in 106 appearances for the club. Clem Stephenson was one of the club's greatest players, gaining two FA Cup winners' medals, in 1913 and 1920, before joining Huddersfield Town where he was an important member of the club's championship-winning sides of 1924–25 and 1925–26. His brother George also played for Villa and went on to win more international caps than Clem. Bruce and Neil Rioch joined Villa from Luton Town in July 1969. Though Bruce appeared in 175 games for Villa between 1969 and 1974 and Neil appeared in 22 games, the brothers played together on only nine occasions.

BROWN, ARTHUR. After playing junior football with Aston Cross, Aston Unity and Aston Comrades, Arthur Brown joined Villa in 1878 but within weeks had left to play for Mitchell St Georges. He also played for Birchfield Trinity and the Excelsior club before returning to Villa in 1880. Known as Digger, he appeared in 22 of the club's first 25 FA Cup ties, scoring 15 goals from either the outside-right or centre-forward position. In 1882 he played for England against Ireland, Scotland and Wales, scoring four goals on his debut as the Irish were beaten 13–0 in Belfast. Unfortunately, he did not play for Villa in the Football League, having to retire through ill-health in 1886.

BROWN, GEORGE. A miner at Mickley Colliery, Northumberland, George Brown asked Huddersfield Town manager Herbert Chapman for a trial and impressed enough to be signed. He helped Huddersfield win three successive league championships and in 1925–26 scored 35 goals. With the Leeds Road club, he won eight England caps and an FA Cup runners-up medal when they lost 3–1 to Blackburn Rovers in 1928. Joining Villa in the summer of 1929, Brown was equally at home at inside- or centre-forward and in his first season scored 30 goals in 41 league games, including hat-tricks against Arsenal (home 5–2) and Everton (home 5–2) plus another in the FA Cup against Blackburn Rovers (home 4–1). On 2 January 1932, Bomber Brown as he was known scored five of Villa's goals in an 8–3 win over Leicester City at Filbert Street. He added another England cap to his collection when he played against Wales in 1933 but in October of the following year he joined Burnley. He spent just one season at Turf Moor before transferring to Leeds United, where he scored 21 goals in 41 matches, later ending his involvement with the game after two years as player-manager of Darlington.

BUCKLEY, CHRIS. The brother of Major Frank Buckley, the famous manager of Wolverhampton Wanderers, Chris Buckley joined Brighton and Hove Albion in 1905 before signing for Aston Villa a year later. Making his debut in a 2–0 win at Stoke on 3 September 1906, he played in 20 games that season and had made the centre-half spot his own when he broke his ankle in the opening game of the 1907–08 season. Out of action for over 12 months, he returned to win a first division championship medal and play in 143 first-team games before he was sold to Woolwich Arsenal in the summer of 1913. After the war, he played in non-league football but in 1936 he was elected to the Villa board and later became chairman.

BURROWS, HARRY. One of the hardest strikers of a dead ball, Harry Burrows made his Villa debut in a 1–0 win at Hull City on Boxing Day 1959. It was his only game in the first team that season, but after some outstanding performances early in the 1961–62 campaign, he made the Number 11 shirt his own. He won a League Cup winners' tankard in 1961 and a runners-up medal in 1963, the season he played for England Under-23s against Greece. Quite a prolific scorer for a winger, 73 in 181 League and Cup games for Villa, he scored a blistering hat-trick in Villa's 4–0 win at Blackpool on 7 September 1963. He left Villa

Park in March 1965, transferring to a Stoke City side for whom he scored 69 goals in 245 league appearances. He later joined Plymouth Argyle but after helping the Home Park club win promotion to the second division in 1974–75, injury forced his retirement from the game.

C

CALLAGHAN, ERNIE. Spotted by John Devey whilst playing for Atherstone Town, Ernie 'Mush' Callaghan made his Villa debut in the FA Cup third-round replay win over Bradford City in January 1933. Initially partnering George Cummings at full-back, he later switched to centre-half and was an ever-present in 1938–39. Like a lot of other professionals, his career was cruelly interrupted by the Second World War. During the hostilities he served with the Police Reserve and in 1941 played for the National Police side against the RAF at Wembley. In 1942, Callaghan was awarded the BEM for bravery during the Birmingham Blitz and three years later won a War League Cup tankard as Villa beat Blackpool. He played for just one season when league

Ernie Callaghan

27

football resumed before retiring to become the club's maintenance man!

CAMPBELL, JOHNNY. The scorer of the first-ever goal at Villa Park when the Villans beat Blackburn Rovers 3–0 on 15 April 1897, Johnny Campbell joined the club in 1895 from Glasgow Celtic. At Parkhead, Campbell once scored 12 goals in a game playing for Celtic's reserve side in a pre-season friendly. In his two seasons at Villa before he returned to Celtic, the club won two league championships and the FA Cup. Campbell's excellent dribbling skills and strong shot earned him 43 goals in 63 games, including four goals in his second game in a 7–3 win over Small Heath. After returning to Scotland, he added to his collection – three Scottish FA Cup winners' medals and three league championship medals, another league championship medal with Third Lanark, whom he joined in 1903, and 12 Scottish caps.

CAPACITY. The total capacity of Villa Park during the 1996–97 season was 39,339, all seated.

CAPEWELL, LEN. Len Capewell served with the Royal Engineers in Belgium in the First World War. He returned to these shores to play non-league football for Wellington Town before signing for Aston Villa in the summer of 1920. He scored on his debut at Blackburn Rovers as Villa won 2–1 and over the next six seasons or so proved himself to be a prolific goalscorer. He scored five goals in Villa's 10-0 win over Burnley on the opening day of the 1925–26 season, four against Port Vale in a 7–2 FA Cup win and a hat-trick whilst suffering from a dislocated shoulder at home to Everton in December 1926. He scored exactly 100 goals for Villa in 156 league and Cup matches before ending his league career with Walsall, eventually returning to play for Wellington Town in 1931.

CAPS. The most capped player in the club's history is Paul McGrath who won 51 caps for the Republic of Ireland during his stay at Villa Park between August 1989 and August 1996.

CAPS (ENGLAND). The first Villa player to be capped by England was Howard Vaughton, when he played against Ireland in 1882. The most capped England player is David Platt with 22 caps.

CAPS (NORTHERN IRELAND). The first Villa player to be capped by Northern Ireland was William Renneville, when he played against Wales in 1911. The most capped Northern Ireland player is Peter McParland with 33 caps.

CAPS (SCOTLAND). The first Villa player to be capped by Scotland was James Cowan when he played against England in 1886. The most capped Scotland player is Alex Massie with 7 caps.

CAPS (WALES). The first Villa player to be capped by Wales was Willie Evans when he played against England in 1892. The most capped Wales player is Leighton Phillips with 26 caps.

CAPTAINS. George Ramsay led the club to their first trophy success in 1880 when they won the Birmingham Senior Cup. When Archie Hunter was captain, the club once chartered a special train just to take him to Nottingham. Hunter was an amateur and his employer would not let him leave early for matches. In fact, in his early days he played under an assumed name to avoid trouble at work. Hunter was the first player to receive the FA Cup in 1887; he scored the second goal in the final against West Bromwich Albion. John Devey was another great captain and he led Villa to five League Championships and two FA Cup successes. 'The Prince of Full-backs', Howard Spencer led Villa to victory in the 1905 FA Cup final over Newcastle United, whilst Jimmy Harrop who had played brilliantly when Villa won the FA Cup in 1913 was injured for the 1920 final and was replaced by Andy Ducat who led the club to a 1–0 win over Huddersfield Town. Johnny Dixon was one of Villa's stars of the post-war era and it was he who skippered Villa to victory over Manchester United in the FA Cup final of 1957. When Villa won the league championship in 1981, captain Dennis Mortimer was one of seven players who appeared in all 42 league matches that season. More recently, Andy Townsend led the club to victory over Leeds United in the Football League Cup final of 1996.

CARRODUS, FRANK. Starting his career with his home-town club Altrincham, Frank Carrodus moved into league football in November 1969 with Manchester City. He appeared in 49 first-team games for the Maine Road club before joining Aston Villa in the summer of 1974. In his first season with the club, he helped them win promotion to the first division and picked up a League Cup winners' medal after Villa had beaten Norwich City 1–0 at Wembley. Carrodus won a second League Cup winners' medal in 1977 as Villa beat Everton over three matches. He played in 197 league and Cup games for Villa before moving to Wrexham in December 1979. The likeable midfielder had spells with Birmingham City and Bury before leaving to play non-league soccer.

CASCARINO, TONY. Signed for Gillingham from non-league side Crockenhill in exchange for a team kit! Over the next five seasons his goalscoring exploits in the third division led to him winning the first of 51 caps for the Republic of Ireland and in June 1987 to Millwall parting with their record transfer fee. Forming a deadly partnership with Teddy Sheringham, he helped the Lions to win the second division championship but joined Villa in March 1990 for £1.5 million when it became apparent that the London club were doomed to relegation. The Irish international failed to make an impact at Villa Park, scoring just 11 goals in 46 league appearances. He was transferred to Celtic in the close season of 1991 but found difficulty settling there and the following February, Liam Brady allowed him to join Chelsea.

CENTENARY. Aston Villa celebrated their centenary in 1974 after a disappointing season which saw them finish 14th in the second division. They reached the fifth round of the FA Cup after hanging on with ten men for a draw at Highbury in the previous round. The club appointed a new manager in the summer of 1974 in the shape of Vic Crowe and in 1974–75 he led the club to promotion to the first division and League Cup success at Wembley.

CENTURIES. There are seven instances of individual players who have scored 100 or more league goals for Aston Villa. Harry Hampton is the greatest goalscorer with 215 strikes in his Villa career (1904–1920). Other centurions are Billy Walker (214), John Devey (169), Joe Bache (168), Eric Houghton (160), Tom Waring (159) and Johnny Dixon (132). Gordon Cowans holds the club record for the most consecutive league appearances – 168. Other players to have made over 100 consecutive appearances during their careers are Alec Talbot (136), Ian Ross (127), Charlie Aitken (126), Jimmy Rimmer (125), Des Bremner (107), Les Smith (107), Jimmy Rimmer in a second spell (104) and Charlie Wallace (102).

CHAMPIONSHIPS. Aston Villa have won the league championship on seven occasions. The first time was 1893–94 when they scored 84 goals in their 30 matches. John Devey was top scorer with 20. The club's biggest win in that season, which saw them finish six points clear of runners-up Sunderland, was 9–0 at home to Darwen on Boxing Day. Villa won the league championship for a second time in 1895–96. After beating West Bromwich Albion 1–0 on the opening day of the season, they defeated rivals Small Heath 7–3 with Johnny Campbell netting four of the goals. He ended the season, in which the club only lost five games, as top scorer with 26 goals. The following season Villa not only won the league championship but also the FA Cup, to become the second club after Preston North End to achieve the double. They took the Championship by finishing 11 points clear of runners-up Sheffield United. After a slow start Villa, who had virtually the same side as the previous season, began to find their form. In fact, apart from two games at the beginning of January, Villa were undefeated in their last 25 matches. Fred Wheldon was the club's top scorer with 18 goals, including a superb hat-trick in a 5–1 win at Blackburn Rovers. Villa eventually clinched the title in the 1896–97 season with a magnificent 6–2 win over Bolton Wanderers at Villa Park, this after they had been two goals down at half-time. Villa's fourth league championship success came in 1898–99. They were undefeated at home, winning 15 and drawing two of their matches, including 7–1 victories over Derby County and West Bromwich Albion and a 6–1 win over Notts County. Villa won the title on the last day of the season when a crowd of 41,000 saw their nearest rivals Liverpool beaten 5–0, with all the goals coming in the first-half. In 1899–1900, Villa won the title for the second year in succession. A 1–0 win at Sunderland on the opening day of the season was followed by a 9–0 rout of Glossop with Billy Garraty scoring four of the goals. Villa took 11 points from their last six matches to beat off a determined challenge from Sheffield United, who finished two points adrift of the champions. The club's sixth league championship came in 1909–10, when they were again unbeaten at home, winning 17 and drawing two of their matches, including beating Manchester United 7-1. Their away form wasn't that good for a Championship-winning side, yet they were five points ahead of Liverpool at the end of the season. Villa last won the league championship in 1980–81, when a 12 match unbeaten run in the autumn set them on their way. They won seven consecutive matches in January and February and reached the last day of a long season needing just a draw against Arsenal at Highbury. An estimated 20,000 Villa fans swelled the gate to 57,472 and though Arsenal won 2–0, it did not matter as the club's nearest rivals Ipswich Town went down at Middlesbrough. Seven Villa players – Bremner, Cowans, McNaught, Morley, Mortimer, Rimmer and Swain – had played in every game.

CHARITY SHIELD. Aston Villa have appeared in the Charity Shield on four occasions:

1911	Brighton and Hove Albion (Stamford Bridge)	0–1
1958	Manchester United (Old Trafford)	0–4
1973	Manchester City (Villa Park)	0–1
1982	Tottenham Hotspur (Wembley)	2–2

The two clubs held the Shield for six months each.

CHARLES, GARY. A stylish right-back with great pace, Gary Charles began his career with Nottingham Forest where he played in 79 first-team games. He joined Derby County in the summer of 1993 for a fee of £750,000, but following the departure of Earl Barrett to Everton, he signed for Villa in January 1995. He made his debut against Nottingham Forest, coming on as a substitute and ended the season with 16 appearances to his name. The following campaign saw him play in a more aggressive role, combining midfield and defensive duties. He played in 34 of the 38 Premier League matches and scored his first goal for the club in the 3–0 win over Southampton in April. He won a League Cup winners' medal and looked likely to add to the two full England caps he won whilst with Forest in 1991 until he suffered a broken ankle.

CHATT, BOB. Bob Chatt began his footballing career with Middlesbrough Ironopolis who were trying to get into the second division of the Football League. After he had scored over 50 goals in four seasons at Ironopolis, Villa were one of a number of clubs chasing his signature. He joined the club in 1893, making his debut in the final game of that season before becoming a regular member of the first team. In the 1895 FA Cup final against West Bromwich Albion, he was credited with scoring after only 39 seconds, still the fastest Cup final goal on record. He gained league championship medals in 1896 and 1897 to add to his winners' medal in that Cup final of 1895. After leaving Villa, he reverted to amateur status and achieved the unique feat of adding an FA Amateur Cup winners' medal to his collection.

CHATTERLEY, LEW. Joining Villa after leaving school, Lew Chatterley made his debut for the club against Nottingham Forest in May 1963. Eventually developing into a fine right-half, Chatterley was one of the club's great utility players in his early days, appearing in eight different numbered outfield shirts. In 1966–67 when Villa were relegated to the second division, he was the club's top scorer with 13 goals and the following season was ever present. He left Villa Park in September 1971, after appearing in 164 first-team games, to join Northampton Town. Chatterley spent just one season with the Cobblers before moving to Grimsby Town. In March 1974, after playing in 75 games for the Blundell Park side, he transferred to Southampton where he managed just nine league games before ending his playing career with Torquay United. He had played in a total of 324 league games, scoring 54 goals. He later had two spells at The Dell as senior coach.

CHESTER, REG. After trials with Notts County and Mansfield Town, Reg Chester joined Peterborough before later moving to Stamford Town. It was whilst playing for Stamford that he was spotted by a Villa scout and in April 1925 he signed professional forms for the club. He arrived at Villa Park as a centre-forward. Lacking the necessary physique, he was switched to the wing with great success. He was with Villa for ten years and though he could play on either flank, he made only 97 first-team appearances for the club, scoring 34 goals. On 20 April 1929, he scored a hat-trick in Villa's 4–1 win over Huddersfield Town. In August 1935, he joined Manchester United, the club against whom he had made his Villa debut, but after scoring one goal in 13 appearances, he returned to the East Midlands to play with Arnold Town and then Woodborough United.

CLEAN SHEET. This is the colloquial expression used to describe a goalkeeper's performance when he does not concede a goal. Jim Cumbes in 1974–75 kept 18 clean sheets in 35 league appearances, plus another four in FA and League Cup ties. In 1971–72, Cumbes kept 18 clean sheets in just 29 league appearances, whilst Hughes with seven and Crudgington with one on his only appearance, meant that the club had 26 clean sheets in 46 matches as they won the third division championship.

COCA-COLA CUP. See Football League Cup.

COLOUR. Villa's colours are claret shirts with light blue sleeves, light blue and yellow trim, white shorts with a claret and blue trim and claret socks with a light blue trim. Their change colours are white shirts with claret and blue trim, claret shorts, white socks with claret and blue hoop.

CONSECUTIVE HOME GAMES. Aston Villa played an extraordinary, intense sequence of five home games in succession in just 29 days, 6 March – 4 April 1893. They won four of them – Newton Heath (2–0), Notts County (3–1), Accrington (6–4) and Wolverhampton Wanderers (5–0) – but lost the last one 3–1 to Burnley.

CONSECUTIVE SCORING – LONGEST SEQUENCE. Len Capewell holds the club record for consecutive scoring when he was on target in eight consecutive league games. His first came in the 2–2 draw with Manchester United at Villa Park on 7 September 1925 and the sequence ended with the equalising goal in the 3–3 draw at home to Birmingham City on 17 October. In the opening game that season on 29 August, Capewell had scored five goals in the 10–0 thrashing of Burnley.

COWAN, JAMES. James Cowan was the rock around which the

Villa defence of the 1890s was built. He was a skilful tackler and extremely fast. Cowan joined Villa from Vale of Leven in 1889 after George Ramsay had overheard a conversation about Warwick County inviting the Scot to Birmingham for a trial. Making his Villa debut in a 2–2 draw at home to Burnley on the opening day of the 1889–90 season, he soon settled into the side. An ever-present for four of his 13 seasons with the club, he played in 354 league and Cup games, scoring 26 goals. He won two FA Cup winners' medals and five league championship medals. He was capped by Scotland on just three occasions, the miserly total a reflection of the attitude towards Anglo-Scots at the time, rather than the player's ability. His first cap came in 1896 when the Scots beat England 2–1 in Glasgow, their first success in six years. Earlier that year he had returned to his native Scotland and won the famous Powderhall Sprint Handicap, although he was later fined and suspended by the Villa committee who thought he was at home recovering from injury! Retiring in 1902, he had a spell coaching the club's youngsters before becoming Queens Park Rangers first-ever manager.

COWANS, GORDON. One of the most skilful players in the country, Gordon Cowans made his league debut for Villa as a substitute at Manchester City on 7 February 1976. By the end of the following season, he was a regular in the side that finished fourth in the first division and won the League Cup. He remained an automatic choice in midfield for the next six years and from 1979 to 1983 was an ever-present, playing in 168 consecutive matches. In 1980, he was voted Young Player of the Year and the following season inspired Villa to the league championship. Linking well with Dennis Mortimer and Des Bremner, he helped Villa lift the European Cup in 1981–82 and the European Super Cup the following season. He graduated to full England honours when he made his debut against Wales at Wembley in February 1983, the first of his ten full caps. In August of that year, he suffered a double fracture of the right leg which kept him sidelined for the whole of the 1983–84 season. He returned in 1984–85 but failed to recapture his pre-injury form and at the end of the season moved to Italian First Division club Bari for £500,000. After three years in Italy, he returned to Aston Villa in the summer of 1988 and was an ever-present for a fifth season in

Gordon Cowans

1990–91 before being transferred to ambitious Blackburn Rovers. He assisted the Ewood Park club to promotion via the play-offs. At the end of the 1992–93 season he rejoined Villa for a third spell, taking his number of first–team appearances to 527 before joining Derby County and later playing for Wolverhampton Wanderers, Sheffield United and Bradford City.

COX, GERSHOM. Playing his early football with the Excelsior club, Gershom Cox joined Villa in August 1887 and made his debut on the opening day of the Football League competition in September 1888. After having the misfortune to score the first-ever own goal in the competition as Villa drew with Wolves 1–1, he went on to give six years splendid service. A strong-tackling defender, he played in 98 league and Cup games for Villa before joining Willenhall Pickwick in June 1893. He later played for Walsall Brunswick and Bloxwich Strollers before a broken leg forced him to leave the game. He joined the Birmingham City Police Force as a Special Constable and was often to be seen officiating at Villa's home games.

COX, NEIL. After playing in only 17 league games for his local side Scunthorpe United, Neil Cox was signed by Aston Villa manager Jozef Venglos on the recommendation of youth coach, Richard Money. Villa paid a staggering £400,000 for a player with less than six months Football League experience. Cox had to wait more than a year before making his first-team debut at Notts County. Used mainly as full-back cover for Earl Barrett or in midfield, he never let the side down. Chosen for the England Under-21 side, he progressed well and played in 57 first-team games for Villa before being allowed to join Middlesbrough for £1 million in July 1994. Following Boro's relegation in 1996–97 he joined newly-promoted Bolton Wanderers for £1.2 million.

CRABTREE, JIMMY. Jimmy Crabtree was one of the most skilful and versatile players to wear Villa's famous colours of claret and blue, playing in all five defensive positions, apart from goalkeeper, at international level. He joined Villa from Burnley in July 1895 and after making the first of his 200 appearances at full-back alongside Howard Spencer in a 1–0 win against West Bromwich Albion, he was converted into a left-half. He helped the club to four league championships and an FA Cup final win over Everton in 1897. He won 11 of his 14 England caps with Villa and appeared six times for the Football League. He left Villa Park for Oreston Rovers in the summer of 1902 but within a year had joined Plymouth Argyle. He played in only five games for the Pilgrims before rejoining Oreston in August 1904. He retired two years later and returned to live in Birmingham where he died at the surprisingly early age of 36.

CRICKETERS. Seven Aston Villa players have been cricketers of real note. Andy Ducat, who captained Villa to victory in the FA Cup final of 1920, was a highly talented forcing batsman and an outstandingly fast and sure-footed outfielder who played for Surrey from 1906 to 1931. A double international, his only Test match saw him dismissed by Australia's Ted McDonald in a most unusual manner – the express delivery smashed the shoulder off his bat and carried to slip as the splinter dislodged a bail. For Surrey, he scored 23,108 runs at an average of 38.64 and exceeded 1,000 runs in a season on 14 occasions. His highest score was 306 not out, made against Oxford University at The Oval in 1919, the same season that he scored a century before lunch as he and E.G. Hayes shared the county's record third wicket stand of 353 against Hampshire at Southampton. Ducat died of a heart attack while batting at Lord's in a wartime Home Guard match between Surrey and Sussex. John Devey played for Warwickshire between 1894 and 1907, scoring 6,515 runs at an average of 28.20 and capturing 16 wickets. His highest score was 246 made against Derbyshire at Edgbaston in 1900. Other Villa players to represent Warwickshire were Billy George (1901–06) and Eric Houghton, who made his first-class cricket debut against India at Edgbaston in August 1946, some 18 years after he had made his Villa debut. Fred Wheldon played for Worcestershire between 1899 and 1906, scoring 4,938 runs at an average of 22.25. South African-born Gordon Hodgson was a fast bowler for Lancashire, taking 148 first-class wickets at 27.75 runs each. Jim Cumbes, Villa's giant goalkeeper, played first-class cricket for four counties, Surrey, Lancashire, Worcestershire and Warwickshire. He took 379 wickets in a career that spanned 20 years from 1963 to 1983, winning county championship and Gillette Cup winners' medals with Worcestershire.

CROPLEY, ALEX. Although born in Aldershot, Alex Cropley was brought up in Scotland and in 1968 joined Hibernian. At Easter Road he won three Scottish Under-23 caps and was selected at full international level on two occasions. In December 1974, he was transferred to Arsenal for £150,000 but after appearing in just 30 league games for the Gunners, he moved to Villa Park in a £125,000 deal. He made his Villa debut in a 2–0 win over Leicester City in September 1976, ending the season with a League Cup winners' tankard after Everton had been beaten at the third attempt. In December 1977, he broke his leg in Villa's 3–0 win over West Bromwich Albion and was never the same player. He had a loan spell at Newcastle United before leaving Villa Park in September 1981 to join Portsmouth. A year later, he returned to Hibernian before hanging up his boots in 1983–84.

CROWD TROUBLE. However unwelcome, crowd disturbances at major football matches are far from a modern phenomenon. Though behaviour at Villa Park has usually been of a high standard, on one occasion when the club played at Perry Barr one of the most serious incidents of the game's early days took place. On 7 January 1888, a record crowd of 26,849 twice invaded the pitch during the fifth-round FA Cup tie between Villa and Preston North End. To be fair, the pitch invasions were a result of over-crowding rather than misbehaviour by spectators. However, Hussars and mounted police had to be called and Villa, the Cup holders, were disqualified for failing to maintain order.

CROWE, VIC. Though he was born in South Wales, Vic Crowe was just two years old when he moved with his family to Handsworth, Birmingham. After playing with Erdington Albion, West Bromwich's nursery side, he signed professional forms for Aston Villa in the summer of 1952. He made his first-team debut at Manchester City on 16 October 1954 and Tommy Thompson scored a hat-trick in Villa's 4–2 win. In 1959–60, he missed just one game as Villa won the second division championship. He was capped 16 times by Wales, winning his first against England at Villa Park on 26 November 1958 in a 2–2 draw. In 1960–61, he was instrumental in Villa winning the first-ever League Cup and in 1963 won a runners-up prize in the same competition. He left

Villa Park in 1964 to join Peterborough United after appearing in 351 league and Cup matches. He played in just 56 league matches for Posh before becoming assistant coach to NASL side Atlanta Chiefs. He returned to Villa Park in 1969 and in January 1970 became the club's manager. He took them to the League Cup final in 1971 and a year later led the club back into the second division. He left Villa in 1974 to coach Portland Timbers before returning to these shores to coach in non-league soccer.

CUMBES, JIM. Goalkeeper Jim Cumbes turned professional with Tranmere Rovers, helping them win promotion to the third division in his first season. He left Prenton Park in the summer of 1969, joining West Bromwich Albion for £33,350. He spent two years at the Hawthorns playing in 64 league games before signing for Aston Villa for £36,000. Making his debut in a 6–0 win at Oldham Athletic on 27 November 1971, he played in 29 games that season, keeping 18 clean sheets and winning a third division championship medal. An ever-present the following season when Villa finished third in division two, he missed just one game in 1973–74. In 1974–75 he played in all but four of Villa's games as they won promotion to the top flight, and collected a winners' tankard when Villa won the League Cup. He left Villa in March 1976, signing off with a superb display in a 2–0 win over Arsenal. He joined his old Villa boss Vic Crowe at Portland Timbers before returning to this country to play non-league football with Runcorn, Southport, Worcester City and Kidderminster Harriers. A more than useful fast bowler, he played first-class cricket for Surrey, Lancashire, Worcestershire and Warwickshire.

George Cummings

CUMMINGS, GEORGE. A tough-tackling, uncompromising full-back, George Cummings won representative honours with the

Scottish Junior FA before turning professional with Partick Thistle in 1932. He won three caps for Scotland, appeared twice for the Scottish League and toured the USA and Canada in the summer of 1935 with the Scottish FA. In November of that year, he joined Villa for a fee of £9,350, putting pen to paper in a Princes Street café in the centre of Edinburgh. With Villa he won a second division championship medal in 1937–38 and a League Cup (North) winners' tankard in 1944. Also, during the war, he guested for Birmingham City, Falkirk, Northampton Town and Nottingham Forest. He returned to Villa after the hostilities and captained the club until 1949 when he retired after appearing in 232 first-team games for the club.

CUMMINGS, TOMMY. Tommy Cummings made 434 first-team appearances for Burnley after succeeding the Turf Moor side's regular centre-half Alan Brown. He played a leading role in the Clarets winning their second league championship in 1959–60 and gained an FA Cup runners-up medal in 1962 when they lost to Spurs 3–1. Cummings also played for the Football League and won three England B caps. He was chairman of the PFA for two years before he took over as player-manager of Mansfield Town. He almost led the Stags to promotion in his first season but in the summer of 1967 he succeeded Dick Taylor as manager of Aston Villa. He spent 16 largely undistinguished months at Villa Park and in November 1968, with the club languishing at the bottom of the second division, he was sacked.

CUNLIFFE, ARTHUR. One of the game's quickest wingers, Arthur Cunliffe began his league career with Blackburn Rovers in 1928 and spent five years with the club before joining Villa in May 1933. At Ewood Park, he won two England caps and formed a good left-wing partnership with Ronnie Dix, who moved to Villa Park with him. Cunliffe made his debut in the final game of the 1932–33 season, scoring in a 2–0 win over Derby County. He quickly established himself and was a regular member of the Villa side over the next two seasons, in which he scored 13 goals in 75 appearances. In December 1936, he joined Middlesbrough, later playing for Burnley, Hull City and Rochdale. At Spotland, he became first-team trainer, a position he was to hold with Bournemouth from July 1950.

CUPS. Aston Villa has won 21 major trophies: seven league titles; seven FA Cups; five Football League Cups; one European Cup and one European Super Cup.

CURCIC, SASA. He was one of the bargain buys of the 1995–96 season when Bolton Wanderers paid Partizan Belgrade £1.5 million for his services in October 1995. The Yugoslavian international added another dimension to the Wanderers' midfield, though his silky skills were not enough to help them avoid the drop into the first division. He scored some memorable goals, notably in the two matches against Chelsea. He appeared in 33 league and Cup games for the Wanderers before becoming unsettled with the thought of first division football. In the summer of 1996, he joined Aston Villa for a club record fee of £4 million and made his debut in the home game against Derby County, the team he was later to score his first goal for the club against in a fourth-round FA Cup defeat. Disappointed at being left out of the Villa side, it remains to be seen whether his future lies at Villa Park.

D

DALEY, TONY. On his day Tony Daley was one of the most exciting wingers in the Football League. He arrived at Villa Park straight from school and signed full-time forms in May 1985, a month after making his League debut at Southampton. An instant hit with the fans, he suffered the disappointment of relegation to the second division at the end of his first full season. Injuries and loss of form kept him out of the side until midway through the 1987–88 season when he returned to score three vital goals as Villa climbed back into the first division. Injuries again disrupted his career in 1990–91 but the following

Tony Daley

season, under Ron Atkinson, he held down a regular place and won his first England cap as a substitute in the vital European Championship qualifying game in Poland. He went on to appear in seven internationals for England, playing his last game against Sweden in the European Championship finals of 1992. The following two seasons saw him in and out of the Villa side and in June 1994 after playing in 290 first-team matches for the Villa Park club he joined neighbours Wolverhampton Wanderers for £1.25 million. However, due to injuries he had to wait a year before making his debut.

DEAKIN, ALAN. After making his Villa debut against Rotherham United a month after his 18th birthday, Alan Deakin had to wait until the following season of 1960–61 to win a regular place in the Villa line-up. At the start of the following campaign, he won a League Cup winners' tankard as Villa beat Rotherham United 3–2 over two legs. His form was very impressive around this time and he won six England Under-23 caps before having the misfortune to break his ankle during the 1964–65 season. He fought his way back to reclaim his rightful place in the side, captaining the club in 1966–67, a season which unfortunately saw them relegated. He played in 270 first-team games for Villa before joining Walsall in October 1969. He played in 50 league games for the Saddlers before moving into non-league football.

DEATH. Archie Hunter was playing centre-forward for Aston Villa against Everton at Anfield on 4 January 1890 when he collapsed suffering from a heart attack. He was taken to hospital but never fully recovered and died four years later, aged 35. Tommy Ball was shot dead by his policeman neighbour when he was only 24 years old. Signed from Newcastle United, he had played in 77 league and Cup games for Villa and was being groomed to replace Frank Barson. Andy Ducat, who was a double international at football and cricket, captained Villa in the 1920 FA Cup final. He died playing cricket at Lord's in 1942, aged 56.

DEBUTS. One of the club's most unusual debuts occurred when goalkeeper Harry Morton, who was a spectator in the stand at Maine Road, was called upon to play. Regular keeper Fred Biddlestone had injured himself during the pre-match kick-in. Morton performed heroics as Villa drew 3–3 with Manchester City, and went on to play in 207 league and Cup games for Villa.

DEEHAN, JOHN. A striker who did his fair share of creating goals as well as scoring them, John Deehan formed splendid partnerships with both Andy Gray and Brian Little during his time at Villa Park. He helped the club win the League Cup in 1977 and won seven England Under-21 caps, but after just six games of the 1979–80 season, he left to join West Bromwich Albion. Unfortunately, the move did not work out and in December 1981 he was transferred to Norwich City for £175,000. At Carrow Road, Deehan scored 65 goals in just under 200 first-team matches,

John Deehan

winning a League Cup winners' medal in 1985 and a second division championship medal the following year. When he left Norwich he stayed in East Anglia, signing for Ipswich Town. He helped the Portman Road club into the division two promotion play-offs before ending his playing days with Manchester City and Barnsley. Deehan worked as a coach with Manchester City, Barnsley and Norwich City before becoming manager at Carrow Road in 1994. The Canaries were at the time adopting a policy of selling their best players, so in November 1995 he resigned, taking over as manager of Wigan Athletic.

DEFEATS – FEWEST. During the 1896–97 season, Villa suffered only four defeats in the 30 match programme. They won the first division championship.

DEFEATS – MOST. Aston Villa's total of 24 defeats during the 1966–67 season is the worst in the club's history. Not surprisingly, they finished next to the bottom of the first division and were relegated.

DEFEATS – WORST. Villa have lost five first division matches

7–0. Blackburn Rovers (away 1889–90), Everton (away 1889–90), West Bromwich Albion (home 1935–36), Manchester United (away 1949–50) and Manchester United again (away 1964–65). On 2 March 1889, Villa lost 8–1 at Blackburn Rovers in a third-round FA Cup match.

DEFENSIVE RECORDS. Villa's best defensive record was established in 1971–72 and equalled in three other seasons. They conceded just 32 goals in each of those seasons, winning the third division championship in 1971–72 and finishing as runners-up in the second division in 1974–75. Villa's worst defensive record was in 1935–36 when they conceded 110 goals to finish 21st in the first division and were relegated.

DERBIES. The rivalry between Aston Villa and Birmingham City has become an established part of the Football League scene. Birmingham were originally known as Small Heath Alliance from their formation in 1875 until 1888 when they dropped 'Alliance'. In 1905 they became Birmingham and added City in 1945. Of the 96 league meetings between them, Villa have won 39 and Birmingham 32 with 25 drawn. Villa have completed the double i.e. won both league games in a season, on eight occasions, the Blues on five. The two clubs first met in the Football League at Perry Barr on the opening day of the 1894–95 season. Villa won 2–1 with goals from Smith and Gordon. The following season, Villa completed the first of their eight doubles over their rivals, winning 7–3 at home and 4–1 away. In the first game, Johnny Campbell scored four of Villa's goals, while John Devey scored two in each game. The games were usually hard fought and on 24 March 1923, Billy Walker converted two penalties in Villa's 3–0 win, penalties awarded due to the robust tackling of the visitors! Gerry Hitchens scored a hat-trick in the Villa Park clash of 1960–61 as the Villans won 5–1 and scored one at St Andrews in the return which ended all-square. The last time the clubs met in the league was at St Andrews on 12 December 1987 when two Garry Thompson goals gave Villa a 2–1 win.

DEVEY, JOHN. Joining Villa in March 1891, John Devey was a highly skilled individualist who in 11 years as a player with the club, won five league championship medals and two FA Cup winners' medals. He scored two goals on his debut in a 5–1 home win over Blackburn Rovers on the opening day of the 1891–92 season and, in fact, scored seven goals in his first four outings. He ended his first season at Villa Park as leading goalscorer with 34 goals in 30 appearances, including four in the 12–2 win over Accrington and a hat-trick in the 6–1 victory over Burnley. A contemporary of Steve Bloomer and John Goodall, one of Devey's greatest disappointments was that he did not play for England against Scotland, his two international appearances being poor reward for his skilful play, knowledge of the game and goalscoring ability. John Devey was also a more than useful cricketer, scoring 6,515 runs for Warwickshire between 1888 and 1907. His best season was 1906, four years after he had retired from football, when he scored 1,237 runs. His top score of 246 was made against Derbyshire at Edgbaston in 1900. After scoring 187 goals in 306 appearances and topping the club's goalscoring charts in six seasons, he hung up his boots and joined the board, serving the club as a director for over 30 years.

DICKSON, BILLY. A Scottish international, Billy Dickson won his only cap whilst playing for Dundee Strathmore. He played against Ireland in Belfast in March 1888. Amazingly, despite scoring four of his side's goals in their 10–2 win, he was never selected for his country again. Soon after, he joined Sunderland before moving to Villa in the close season of 1889. He was a regular in Villa's first-team for the next three seasons and won a runners-up medal when they were beaten 3–0 by West Bromwich Albion in the FA Cup final of 1892. At the end of that season he joined Stoke where in five seasons at the Victoria Ground he scored 40 goals in 119 league games. At Villa he had scored over a goal every other game and many supporters wondered just why the club let him go.

DISMISSALS. Andy Townsend holds the unenviable record of being the first Aston Villa player to be dismissed in a Premier League match when the Villans played Wimbledon at Selhurst Park on 9 November 1994. Villa lost the game 4–3. Townsend was given his marching orders a second time that season at Villa Park on 17 April 1995 when Arsenal won 4–0. The Villa captain was dismissed a third time on 23 September 1995 in the match against Nottingham Forest at Villa Park which ended all-square at 1–1.

DIX, RONNIE. Ronnie Dix made a goalscoring league debut for Bristol Rovers against Norwich City on 3 March 1928 when only 15 years 180 days old, which made him the youngest-ever Football League scorer. In May 1932, he moved to Blackburn Rovers but within a year he and his left-wing partner, Arthur Cunliffe, joined Aston Villa. He made his debut in the last game of the 1932–33 season and over the next season was a regular member of the Villa Park side. Never a prolific scorer, he did score seven goals in the space of three games in 1936–37, including a hat-trick in a 4–0 win over Swansea Town. After scoring 30 goals in 104 league and Cup games he moved on to Derby County. It was while he was at the Baseball Ground that he won his only England cap, scoring in a 4–0 win over Norway. He moved to Tottenham Hotspur in the summer of 1939 before ending his career with Reading. During the war, he guested for a number of clubs, winning a League Cup (North) winners' medal with Blackpool in 1943 and a runners-up medal in the same competition the following year when Villa beat the Seasiders 5–4 on aggregate.

DIXON, JOHNNY. Spotted during the Second World War playing for Spennymoor United, Johnny Dixon joined Aston Villa in the summer of 1944. Though he played in a few wartime games, he had to wait until the opening game of the 1946–47 season for his League baptism. He topped the club's scoring list in four of his seasons at Villa Park, with a best of 26 in 42 league matches in 1951–52 when Villa finished sixth in the first division. Dixon was Villa's captain when they won the FA Cup in 1957 and though he played in only four games of the club's second division championship winning season of 1959–60, he played an important role off the field in encouraging the younger members of the squad. He played his last game for Villa against Sheffield Wednesday on 29 April 1961, scoring one of the goals in a 4–1 win. Unfortunately for the popular Dixon, he ended the game with a broken nose. After retiring from playing, Dixon spent six years at Villa Park coaching the club's youngsters.

DOCHERTY, TOMMY. One of the best-known managers in soccer, Tommy Docherty began his playing career with Preston North End, appearing in 324 out of a possible 356 league games.

He missed 21 through injury and seven through being called upon by Scotland. He moved to Arsenal but had the misfortune to break a leg when playing for the Gunners at Preston. He became senior coach at Chelsea but played in four league games during an emergency. In September 1961, he became caretaker manager when Ted Drake parted company with the club and a few months later his appointment was confirmed on a permanent basis. Under his guidance, the young Chelsea side reached the FA Cup semi-finals three seasons in succession, going to Wembley in 1967, only to lose 2–1 to Spurs. One of the game's most controversial characters, he was an outspoken and much travelled manager. He left Stamford Bridge to manage Rotherham United, then had 28 days in charge of Queens Park Rangers. He was due to take over as team chief at Atletico Bilbao but before he went the Aston Villa directors asked him to help them out. Appointed in December 1968, Docherty's side just avoided relegation from the second division after losing only five of their last 23 games. The following season was one of the worst in Villa's history and in January 1970 with the club bottom of the second division, he was sacked. After a spell with Porto, he was appointed Scotland's team manager before succeeding Frank O'Farrell at Old Trafford. In four and a half seasons with Manchester United, he assembled an exciting side but after winning the FA Cup in 1977, he was dismissed and with it went his best chance of major managerial success. Docherty is now an entertaining after-dinner speaker with engagements world wide.

DORIGO, TONY. Tony Dorigo emigrated from Australia to sign associated schoolboy forms for Aston Villa in January 1982 before being apprenticed eight months later. He made his league debut for Villa at Ipswich Town in the final game of the 1983–84 season, claiming a regular place over the next couple of seasons. When Villa were relegated from the first division at the end of the 1986–87

Tony Dorigo

49

season, Dorigo joined Chelsea for £475,000 but at the end of his first season at Stamford Bridge, they too were relegated. His only goal for Villa in 133 league and Cup games came in a 4–1 home win over Watford, yet for Chelsea he scored 11 league goals and the only goal of the game when Chelsea beat Middlesbrough in the 1990 Zenith Data Systems Cup final. He made the first of his 15 appearances for England against Yugoslavia in 1989 and in 1991 joined Leeds United for £1.3 million. He played an outstanding role in the Elland Road club's unexpected league championship success in 1991–92 and in a continuing career with the Yorkshire club, he has appeared in over 200 games.

DORRELL, ARTHUR. Son of former player, Billy Dorrell, Arthur served in the Army during the First World War and as an athlete won the 100 metres sprint final in the French athletics championships of 1915–16. After the war, he signed for Villa and made his league debut at Derby County in September 1919. At the end of his first season, he won an FA Cup winners' medal, replacing Harold Edgley who had broken his leg against Chelsea just three weeks before the final. He represented the Football League against the Irish League in 1922 and 1925 and was unlucky not to win more than four international caps for England. Dorrell formed a notable left-wing partnership with Billy Walker and went on to serve Villa until 1931. Having played in 390 first-team games, scoring 65 goals, he joined Port Vale for a season before retiring from the game.

DORSETT, DICKIE. Dickie Dorsett began his league career with Wolverhampton Wanderers and scored their goal in the 4–1 FA Cup final defeat by Portsmouth in 1939. A goalscoring inside-left, he scored four goals against Leicester City and Everton in a total of 76 in 110 matches for the Molineux club. Though he guested for a number of clubs during the Second World War, including Liverpool, Brentford and Southampton, he was a member of the Wolves side that beat Sunderland in the 1942 Wartime League Cup final. He left Molineux in 1946 to join Villa but by now was a tough-tackling wing-half or left-back, though he did score 36 goals in 271 games for the club. Making his Villa debut in a 1–1 draw at home to Portsmouth, he ended the season as the club's top scorer with 13 goals. He retired from the playing side of the game at the end of the 1952–53 season, but stayed at Villa Park to coach the club's A team. A few years later he joined Liverpool as their assistant trainer before returning to work in the Midlands.

DOUBLE-WINNERS. The double season of 1896–97 began quite modestly for Villa, the defending league champions, winning two and losing two of their first six games, but then a run of ten matches without defeat moved them towards the top of the table. Early in the New Year, they suffered a minor set-back, losing twice in succession, but from the middle of January, the club went through the rest of the season undefeated in league and Cup, with 15 wins and three draws. The league championship was won with four matches to spare, Villa eventually finishing 11 points clear of runners-up Sheffield United. In the FA Cup final, which is widely regarded as one of the best ever, Villa took the lead against Everton, but had to come from a goal behind to snatch a 3–2 win at Crystal Palace ground in front of a then record crowd of 65,000. Another momentous event in this eventful season came in April 1897, when, having already secured the double, Aston Villa moved to a new ground and celebrated in style with a 3–0 win over Blackburn Rovers. Known at first as the Lower Grounds, it was soon renamed Villa Park and, of course, is now one of the top venues in the country.

DOUGAN, DEREK, Born in Belfast, Derek Dougan started his career as a centre-half and was capped for Ireland at schoolboy level before joining Distillery, where he won youth and amateur recognition for his country. Switching to centre-forward, he joined Portsmouth in the summer of 1957 but after just 33 games for the Fratton Park club, he left to play for first division Blackburn Rovers. At Ewood Park, he scored 25 goals in 59 league matches and was in the Blackburn side that lost the 1960 FA Cup final to Wolverhampton Wanderers. Following Gerry Hitchens' departure to Inter Milan, Villa splashed out £15,000 for the popular Irishman's services in August 1961. After making his debut in the opening game of the 1961–62 season, he suffered various injuries but nonetheless scored 12 goals in 27 appearances during that campaign. The following season he won three of his 43 caps for Northern Ireland and scored his only hat-trick for the club in a 6–1 FA Cup win over Peterborough United. He moved

Derek Dougan

to Peterborough United in the summer of 1963, having scored 26 goals in 60 first-team games for Villa. He then had a spell with Leicester City, where he scored 35 goals in 68 league games, before signing for Wolverhampton Wanderers in March 1967 for £50,000. During his time at Molineux, he won a UEFA Cup runners-up medal and a League Cup winners' tankard before leaving the first-class game in 1975. He was chairman of the PFA before returning to Wolves as chairman and chief executive.

DRAPER, MARK. Mark Draper was Leicester City's record signing when they bought him from Notts County for £1.25

million in the summer of 1994. At Meadow Lane, he had appeared in 268 first-team games, scoring 49 goals. Despite the Filbert Street side's struggle, Draper turned in a number of top-class performances. After the arrival of Mark McGhee as manager, he was used in a more attacking midfield role and thus improved his strike rate. He was the subject of a failed £3 million transfer bid from Brian Little on transfer deadline day, but the Villa manager eventually got his man for £3.25 million in July 1995. Draper was quick to make his mark, scoring from long distance on the opening day of the season as Villa beat Manchester United 3–1. On the threshold of an international call up for England, Draper added a touch more creativity to the Villa midfield and thoroughly deserved his League Cup winners' medal in 1996.

DRAWS. Villa played their greatest number of drawn league matches in a single season in 1975–76 when 17 of their matches ended all-square, and their fewest in 1891–92 when not one of their 26 matches were drawn. The club's highest scoring draw is 5-5, a scoreline in two games, one v West Ham United (away 1930–31) and the other v Tottenham Hotspur (away 1965–66).

DUCAT, ANDY. After beginning his career with Southend Athletic, Andy Ducat turned professional with Woolwich Arsenal, making 175 league appearances for the Gunners before joining Aston Villa in June 1912 for £1,000. Though he could play in a variety of positions, Ducat excelled at wing-half. After just four games of the 1912–13 season, he broke his leg and had to sit out the 1913 FA Cup final. Luck was on his side in 1920, when Jimmy Harrop was injured and Ducat captained Villa to victory in the FA Cup final over Huddersfield Town. Already capped whilst at Highbury, he won a further three caps whilst with Villa and was a double international, appearing in a Test match against Australia in 1921. He left Villa in 1921 to play for Fulham and to be near his beloved Surrey Cricket Club, for whom he scored 23,108 runs between 1906 and 1931. He also managed Fulham and played as an amateur with the London Casuals club. Ducat died in July 1942 whilst batting for Surrey Home Guard against Sussex Home Guard at Lord's.

DUGDALE, JIMMY. Turning professional with West Bromwich Albion in 1952, the Liverpool-born defender played in 63 league games for the Hawthorns club before joining Villa for £25,000 in February 1956. With Villa he won an FA Cup winners' medal in 1957, a second division championship medal in 1960 and a League Cup winners' tankard in 1961. Though he never won a full international cap, he played for England B and the Football League during his time with Albion. He played in 254 league and Cup games for Villa, before signing for Queens Park Rangers in October 1962. Sadly, seven months later, injury forced his retirement from the game.

E

EDGLEY, HAROLD. Joining Villa from Crewe Alexandra in June 1911, Harold Edgley found it difficult to break into the first-team until the 1913–14 season when Albert Hall joined Millwall and Charlie Wallace switched flanks to play on the right wing. After the war, he played in every round of the FA Cup competition, scoring in Villa's 3–1 win over Chelsea in the semi-final before cruelly breaking a leg three weeks before they were due to meet Huddersfield Town in the final. The club obtained special permission to present Edgley with a souvenir winners' medal after Villa had won 1–0. He never wore the claret and blue of Villa again, for after recovering from that injury, he joined Queens Park Rangers before ending his league career with Stockport County.

EDWARDS, GEORGE. Signed from Norwich City in the summer of 1938, George Edwards chipped a bone in his ankle in a tackle with Bob Iverson during training which delayed his debut for over two months. In fact, Edwards always played with his ankle heavily strapped following this injury but it did not stop him from serving Villa until the end of the 1950–51 season. During the war, he guested for a number of clubs but still found time to score 95 goals for Villa in 125 matches, with 39 of them coming in just 35 appearances in the Football League (South) in 1945–46. Twice during that season he netted four goals, in victories over Luton Town (7–1) and Arsenal (5–1). He was the club's leading goalscorer in the first two seasons of league football played after the war and holds the record for the second-fastest goal ever by a Villa player when he netted just 13½ seconds into the FA Cup thriller on 10 January 1968 against Manchester United which Villa lost 6–4. After leaving Villa he played non-league football for Bilston United before hanging up his boots in 1955.

EHIOGU, UGO. After coming through the junior ranks at West Bromwich Albion, Ugo Ehiogu made his debut as a substitute at Hull City in September 1990. He appeared once more as a substitute that season before Villa stepped in and signed him just before the start of the 1991-92 campaign. Included in the Villa squad from the word go, he made his debut in the 3–1 win over Arsenal on 24 August 1991. At the end of that first season in which he made seven further league appearances, he was called up to the England Under-21 squad, making his international debut at the end of the season and later captaining them. Over the next two seasons, he only made the starting line-up on a handful of occasions due to the fine form of McGrath and Teale but in 1994–95, he appeared in all but three of the Premiership matches and after winning his first full international cap, he is now a permanent fixture in the Villa side.

EIRE. The first Aston Villa player to be capped by the Republic of Ireland was Tommy Muldoon when he played against Italy in 1926. The most capped player in Villa's history is Paul McGrath who won 51 caps whilst with the club.

ELLIOTT, PAUL. Starting his career with Charlton Athletic, Paul Elliott stayed in the team for two seasons until severe financial pressures forced the club to sell him to Luton Town. At Kenilworth Road he was a first-team regular for two full seasons until Villa decided that he was the man to replace the injured Brendan Ormsby. He played in 69 first-team games for Villa. Reading the game well, he proved dangerous at set-pieces and scored seven goals from his position at centre-back. Elliott was lured to Pisa in Italy in the summer of 1987, but at the end of his contract he joined Celtic. After two years at Parkhead, he returned to London, signing for Chelsea for a fee of £1.4 million. Badly injured in the seventh game of the 1992–93 season following a clash with Liverpool's Dean Saunders, he was stretchered off, never to play again.

EURO '96. Villa Park staged the following matches in Euro '96:

10 June	Holland	0	Scotland	0
13 June	Switzerland	0	Holland	2
18 June	Scotland	1	Switzerland	0
23 June (QF)	Czechoslovakia	1	Portugal	0

EUROPEAN CUP. Aston Villa have participated in Europe's premier competition on two occasions. After winning the league championship in 1980–81, Villa faced Valur Reykjavik of Iceland in the first round, winning 7-0 on aggregate. They beat Dynamo Berlin of East Germany on away goals, Dynamo Kiev and then Anderlecht of Belgium, who succumbed to a single Tony Morley goal. The final in Rotterdam against Bayern Munich should have been a one-sided affair, especially after Villa's keeper Jimmy Rimmer had to go off injured after eight minutes. Nigel Spink who had played in only one first-team game for Villa replaced him and thwarted the German side who dominated the first half. Villa took the lead in the 67th minute when Morley jinked round the German right-back Augenthaler, took the ball to the by-line and crossed to Withe, who scored off the post. It proved to be the only goal of the game and Villa showed that inexperience can win the day, as they became the undisputed champions of Europe. When Villa played their first match in defence of the trophy against Turkish club Besiktas on 15 September 1982, there were no paying spectators to watch them win 3–1. This ban was the result of disciplinary action by UEFA. A goalless draw in Turkey saw Villa through to round two, where they beat Dinamo Bucharest 6–2 on aggregate with Gary Shaw grabbing a second-leg hat-trick at Villa Park. Drawn against Juventus in the quarter-final, Villa's grip on the trophy loosened after the Italian side netted a first-minute goal in the first leg at Villa Park. The visitors went on to take a 2–1 lead to Turin. Despite a Peter Withe goal in Italy, Juventus did not allow Villa a way back and the holders went out 5–2 on aggregate.

EUROPEAN SUPER CUP. Villa met Barcelona in the final of the European Super Cup over two legs in January 1983. The Spanish giants won 1–0 at the Nou Camp Stadium but Villa won the return leg 3–0 to take the trophy 3–1 on aggregate. Villa's scorers in that second leg were Shaw, Cowans (penalty) and McNaught.

EVANS, ALBERT. Albert Evans spent ten years with Villa, winning three league championships and an FA Cup winners' medal. He had the misfortune to break his leg five times – three times with Villa, once with West Bromwich Albion, whom he joined in 1906 and once in a charity game in 1915. Forming one of the club's youngest full-back pairings with Howard Spencer, Evans went on to play in 203 league and Cup games for Villa before joining the Baggies. Though he never won international honours, he represented the Football League against the Irish League in 1900. After three years playing for West Bromwich Albion, he became their trainer, taking over as manager of Coventry City in 1920. Resigning in 1924, Evans travelled the world trying a variety of jobs, including prospecting for gold in the Yukon.

EVANS, ALLAN. Allan Evans began his professional career as a centre-forward for Dunfermline Athletic and scored two hat-tricks for the Pars before he signed for Aston Villa in the summer of 1977. Spending much of his first season at the club in the Central League side, he continued to play up front and scored a double hat-trick in a match against Sheffield United Reserves at Villa Park. He scored for Villa in his third first-team match at Newcastle United but after that he was moved into defence. Though he played quite brilliantly over the next ten seasons or so in his new

Allan Evans

position, he still scored his fair share of goals as he supported the attack. Evans was instrumental in Villa's success of the early '80s and won league championship, European Cup and European Super Cup medals. He also won four full caps for Scotland, his first against Holland in 1982. He helped Villa to win promotion to the first division in 1987–88 but the following season saw him play the last of his 469 games for the club and in 1990 he was released. He had a brief spell in Australia before returning to these shores as assistant-manager to Brian Little at Leicester City. Evans moved back to Villa Park as Little's right-hand man during the 1994–95 season.

EVANS, ALUN. Alun Evans became Britain's first £100,000 teenaged footballer when he joined Liverpool from Wolverhampton Wanderers in September 1968. He had turned professional with the Molineux club in 1966 and scored four league goals in 22 outings before he moved to Anfield. He scored on his Liverpool debut against his old club but then everything seemed to go wrong for him. He was involved in a fracas at a nightclub, ending the evening with a scarred face, and had to undergo a cartilage operation almost immediately afterwards. After scoring 33 goals in 110 league and Cup games, he signed for Villa for a fee of £72,000 in the summer of 1972. He started well at Villa Park but as his form began to deteriorate, he lost his place and after 17 goals in 72 first-team games, he joined Walsall. He had three seasons with the Saddlers before going abroad to play, first in the NASL and then in Australia, before leaving the game in 1980.

EVER-PRESENTS. There have been 62 Aston Villa players who have been ever present throughout a Football League season. The greatest number of ever-present seasons by a Villa player is five by Charlie Aitken and Gordon Cowans. When Villa won the first division championship in 1980–81, they had seven players who played in every match: Jimmy Rimmer, Kenny Swain, Ken McNaught, Des Bremner, Gordon Cowans, Dennis Mortimer and Tony Morley.

F

FA CUP. Aston Villa first participated in the FA Cup in December 1879 when they were drawn away to Stafford Road FC, the Wolverhampton works team, who had lost only three matches in five years. Villa drew 1–1 to earn a replay at Perry Barr, where they won 3–2. Drawn against one of the favourites, Oxford University, who had already appeared in three finals, winning the cup in 1874, the Villa Committee angered its supporters by announcing that the club had scratched. Since then they have gone on to win the trophy on seven occasions. Their first appearance in a final was in 1887 when they beat West Bromwich Albion 2–0 at Kennington Oval.

FA CUP FINALS. Aston Villa have appeared in nine FA Cup finals, winning the trophy on seven occasions.

1887	West Bromwich Albion (Kennington Oval)	2–0
1892	West Bromwich Albion (Kennington Oval)	0–3
1895	West Bromwich Albion (Crystal Palace)	1–0
1897	Everton (Crystal Palace)	3–2
1905	Newcastle United (Crystal Palace)	2–0
1913	Sunderland (Crystal Palace)	1–0
1920	Huddersfield Town (Stamford Bridge)	1–0
1924	Newcastle United (Wembley)	0–2
1957	Manchester United (Wembley)	2–1

FA CUP SEMI-FINALS. Aston Villa have participated in 18 FA
Cup semi-finals up to the end of the 1996–97 season.

FATHER AND SON. Aston Villa have boasted a number of father
and son players, the most notable being Frank Moss senior and
Frank Moss junior, whose brother Amos also played for the club.
Captaining both Villa and England, Frank Moss senior played in
283 first-team games, winning an FA Cup winners' medal in 1920
and appearing in the 1924 final defeat by Newcastle United as
well. His son, Frank Moss junior, also turned in many fine
performances for the club, both at wing-half and centre-half,
playing in 314 League and Cup games before his retirement was
brought forward by an injury sustained in a challenge with
Manchester United's Duncan Edwards. His other son, Amos, a
utility player though preferring to play at wing-half, appeared in
109 first-team games for Villa between 1945 and 1956.

FEWEST DEFEATS. During Villa's first division championship
winning season of 1896–97, the club went through the 30 match
programme losing only four games. The first came at West
Bromwich Albion (1–3) in the second game of the season and the
second at home to Everton (1–2) three weeks later. The club's two
other reversals came in the first two games of the New Year and
in the space of a week, going down at home to Burnley 3–0 and
4–2 against Sunderland at Roker Park.

FINES. In November 1989, the FA fined Aston Villa's Republic of
Ireland international Paul McGrath £8,500 following his remarks
about Manchester United manager Alex Ferguson. It is the
biggest fine imposed by the FA on an individual player.

FIRST DIVISION. Aston Villa have had five spells in the first
division. Founder members of the Football League in 1888, Villa
spent 44 seasons in the first division before being relegated in
1935–36. During that time they won the league championship in
1893–94, 1895–96, 1896–97, 1899–1900 and 1909–10 and
finished as runners-up on eight occasions. Promoted after two
seasons of second division football, the club's second spell in the
top flight lasted 14 seasons, with their highest position being
sixth, achieved in seasons 1947–48, 1951–52 and 1954–55.

Relegated in 1958–59, the club were immediately promoted and spent seven seasons in the first division before relegation to the second and eventually to the third division. It was 1975–76 before Villa played another match in the top flight and during their 12 seasons in the first division in this spell, won the league championship for a sixth time in 1980–81. Relegated in 1986–87, Villa won promotion at the first time of asking and were still in the first division when the new FA Premier League took over in 1992–93.

FIRST LEAGUE MATCH. Aston Villa's first league game was played at Dudley Road on 8 September 1888 against Wolverhampton Wanderers. Wolves kicked downhill in the first half with the sun on their backs although the wind was against them. Early on, Canon and Anderson both went close to scoring for the home side, the latter hitting an upright with Warner in the Villa goal well beaten. Villa replied through Bert Garvey and Arthur Brown. Bayton, the Wolves keeper, denied Green with a last-ditch plunge at the Villa man's feet. After half an hour's play, Wolves took the lead. The ball was crossed into the goal area by Hunter, White put in a header but in trying to clear his line, Villa's full-back Gershom Cox turned it into his own goal to give Wolves a 1–0 advantage. Villa hit back and deservedly drew level shortly before half-time when Tommy Green drove Garvey's pass over the goal line via an upright. In the second half, both sides had chances to take the lead. For Wolves, both Cooper and Hunter had shots saved by Warner, and Anderson missed an open goal from five yards out. Villa's chances fell to Green, Garvey and Albert Allen but the game ended in a 1–1 draw. Villa's team was: J. Warner, J. Coulton, G. Cox, J. Dawson, H. Devey, J. Yates, A. Brown, T. Green, A. Allen, B. Garvey and D. Hodgetts.

FIRST MATCH. Aston Villa's first game was played in March 1875 against Aston Brook St Mary's Rugby Club. The first half which was goalless was played under rugby laws, the second half under Association laws saw Villa win 1–0 with Jack Hughes the scorer. Villa's line-up was: W. Scattergood, W.H. Price, W. Weiss, D.J. Stevens, E.B. Lee, F.G. Matthews, H. Matthews, C.H. Midgely, J. Hughes, W. Such, H. Whateley, G. Page, A.H. Robbins, G. Greaves and T. Page.

FLOODLIGHTS. Villa Park switched on its floodlights for the first time on 25 August 1958 when Villa beat Portsmouth 3–2 in a division one game with goals from Myerscough, Dixon and McParland. The official inauguration of the floodlights was not until 17 November 1958 in a friendly against Hearts.

FOOTBALL LEAGUE. On 2 March 1888, William McGregor, a Scot living in Birmingham, sent out a now famous letter to Blackburn Rovers, Bolton Wanderers, Preston North End, West Bromwich Albion and to the secretary of his own club, Aston Villa, asking them if they would be interested in forming a Football League. Replies to his letter were duly received and an initial meeting was held on the eve of the 1888 FA Cup final. The business was not concluded until 17 April at the Royal Hotel in Manchester, a much more appropriate venue as no southern club had taken any part whatsoever in the initial discussions. It was discovered that no more than 22 dates could actually be set aside for fixtures and so the league itself would have to be restricted to 12 clubs. They were Aston Villa, Derby County, Notts County, Stoke, West Bromwich Albion and Wolverhampton Wanderers from the Midlands; Accrington, Blackburn Rovers, Bolton Wanderers, Burnley, Everton and Preston North End from the north.

FOOTBALL LEAGUE CUP. Not one of the first division clubs to shun the new Football League Cup competition, Aston Villa were the first winners in 1960–61. The final, however, was played at the start of the 1961–62 season. Villa lost the first leg 2–0 to Rotherham United on 22 August but won the Cup 3–0 in extra-time on 5 September. It was the first time that a final of a major domestic competition had been held over from one season to the next. Gerry Hitchens scored 11 goals that season to establish a competition record but he did not play in the final, having joined Inter Milan in the close season. Villa reached the final again in 1962–63, only to lose on aggregate to neighbours Birmingham City. In 1970–71, Villa had a superb run to the League Cup final, beating Manchester United 3–2 on aggregate in the semi-final, before being beaten by Spurs at Wembley by two Martin Chivers goals. Villa reached their fourth League Cup final in 1975 but not before two dramatic semi-final matches against fourth division

The team which took the 1977 Football League Cup

Chester. In the first leg at Sealand Road, the home side were twice behind but snatched a 2–2 draw. At Villa Park, Chester were 2–0 down but rallied to make it 2–2 before a goal from Brian Little ended their dreams. At Wembley, a Ray Graydon goal gave Villa victory over Norwich City, shooting home the rebound after Kevin Keelan had saved his penalty kick. In the 1977 final, Villa were held to a 0–0 draw by Everton. The replay four days later also ended all-square although Everton's Roger Kenyon scored an own goal to cancel out Bob Latchford's scrambled effort. The second replay at Old Trafford provided plenty of excitement.

Everton led with just ten minutes to go; Villa drew level and took the lead a minute later; two minutes after that, Everton forced the game into extra-time. Brian Little scored Villa's winner to end 330 minutes of football – the longest major final ever to have been played in England. In 1994, Villa faced Tranmere Rovers in the semi-final and after losing the first leg 3–1 at Prenton Park, Villa led 2–0 in the return leg. A penalty from John Aldridge after he had been brought down by Mark Bosnich, put Tranmere back in front. Villa's faithful had to wait until two minutes from the end before Dalian Atkinson took the game to a penalty shoot-out.

Bosnich, who many Tranmere fans believed should not have been on the pitch, saved three penalties as Villa won through 5–4. In the final, Villa completely outplayed Manchester United to win 3–1 with Saunders 2, and Atkinson the scorers. Villa's last appearance in the League Cup final came in 1996 when they crushed Leeds United 3–0 with Milosevic, Taylor and Yorke getting the goals. Aston Villa have now played in a record 178 League Cup ties, winning a record 102 matches and drawing 41. Villa's League Cup final scores are:

1961 v	Rotherham United (Millmoor)	2–0
v	Rotherham United (Villa Park)	3–0
1963 v	Birmingham City (St Andrews)	3–1
v	Birmingham City (Villa Park)	0–0
1971 v	Tottenham Hotspur (Wembley)	0–2
1975 v	Norwich City (Wembley)	1–0
1977 v	Everton (Wembley)	0–0
Replay	Everton (Hillsborough)	1–1 (aet)
Replay	Everton (Old Trafford)	3–2 (aet)
1994 v	Manchester United (Wembley)	3–1
1996 v	Leeds United (Wembley)	3–0

FORD, TREVOR. Welsh international Trevor Ford chose to start his league career with his home-town club of Swansea in 1944, despite a number of other clubs, including Cardiff, wanting to sign him. After scoring 44 goals in 41 games for the Swans in the 1945–46 season and nine in the opening six games of the following campaign, Ford left Vetch Field to join Aston Villa. He made his Villa debut in a 2–0 win at Highbury in January 1947 and in nine games that season he scored nine goals. In terms of goals scored his best seasons were 1947–48 and 1949–50 when he netted 18 in each campaign, although on 27 December 1948, he scored four goals

Trevor Ford

as Villa beat Wolves 5-1. In October 1950, Ford left Villa Park after scoring 61 goals in 128 appearances and signed for Sunderland for £30,000. Three years later he joined Cardiff City, one of a number of clubs he had guested for during the Second World War, before playing in Holland for PSV Eindhoven. After a brief spell with Newport County, Ford ended his playing career with non-league Romford.

FOUNDATION. Cricketing enthusiasts of Villa Cross Wesleyan Chapel, Aston, decided to form a football club during the winter months of 1873–74. Football clubs in the Birmingham area were few and far between and so in their first game against Aston Brook St Mary's rugby team, they played one half rugby and the other soccer. In 1876, they were joined by George Ramsay, a Scottish soccer enthusiast who was appointed captain. In a period of less than ten years Ramsay led Aston Villa from obscurity to become one of the country's top clubs.

FRIENDLIES. Villa have played a great number of friendly matches throughout their history, including entertaining the great Brazilian side Santos and their top player, Pele. However, perhaps the best Villa story concerning a friendly match occurred just after the Second World War when Villa were returning by train from a pre-season friendly in Scotland on a hot day in August. The players were feeling very thirsty and Harry Parkes volunteered to dash into the refreshment room at Preston Station, grab a tray of 14 teas and climb aboard again. As the train slowed down, he leapt off and vanished in the direction of the station buffet. Unfortunately, the train did not stop and continued slowly on its journey without him!

FROGGATT, STEPHEN. An exciting young left-winger, Stephen Froggatt made his Villa debut as a substitute on Boxing Day 1991 in the 3–1 home win over West Ham United. He subsequently enjoyed a short run in the first-team and in 1992–93 was capped for the England Under-21 side. That season, he appeared in almost every game until sustaining an ankle injury in the match at Wimbledon. He came back for a couple of games but the injury got the better of him and after playing in 44 league and Cup games for Villa, he signed for Wolverhampton Wanderers in July 1994 for a fee of £1 million.

FULL MEMBERS CUP. Called the Full Members Cup because it was originally open only to first and second division clubs, Villa first entered in 1986–87. Gary Shaw scored two of Villa's goals as they defeated Derby County 4–1 at home in round two. Travelling to Portman Road in round three, Villa went down to the only goal of the game.

G

GAGE, KEVIN. Kevin Gage made his league debut for Wimbledon against Bury on 2 May 1981 and at 17 years 15 days old, is Wimbledon's youngest-ever player. He was instrumental in the club's rise from the fourth division to the top flight, playing in 188 league and Cup games before joining Villa for £100,000 in the summer of 1987. An ever-present in the Villa side that won promotion to the first division in 1987–88, he played in 28 games the following season but struggled to maintain his form when Villa were first division runners-up in 1989–90. Under new manager Ron Atkinson, it became apparent that he had no future at Villa Park and in November 1991, he went on loan to Sheffield United, later signing for the Bramall Lane club for £150,000. He scored for the Blades in the 1–1 draw against Villa later that season. He played in 131 first-team games for the Yorkshire club before joining Preston North End on a free transfer in March 1996.

GARDNER, TOM. Born at Huyton, Tom Gardner made his league debut for Liverpool against Manchester United at Anfield in January 1930, but after just four games he was transferred to Grimsby Town. Within a year, he had left the Mariners and joined Hull City and it was from here that he signed for Aston Villa in February 1934. Making his debut against Stoke City, he went on to play in the last 12 matches that season and was chosen to play for England against Czechoslovakia. In 1934–35, he won a second England cap as he established himself at wing-half in a Villa side that ended the season in mid-table. Injuries marred the rest of his career at Villa Park and in April 1938 he was allowed to leave and joined Burnley. During the war, he guested for a number of clubs including Blackpool, whom he helped win the Wartime League Cup (North) final against Sheffield Wednesday, scoring one of the goals.

GARRATY, BILLY. An important member of the Villa attack, Billy Garraty made his debut towards the end of the 1897–98 season. He was unable to win a regular place in the Villa line-up until the following season, when he scored six goals in the last nine matches, including a hat-trick in the 7–1 win over West Bromwich Albion. His best season with the club was 1899–1900, top-scoring with 27 goals in 33 league appearances, as Villa won the first division championship. That season he scored four goals in Villa's 9–0 win against Glossop and hat-tricks in the 4–2 win over Sunderland and the 6–2 defeat of Notts County. Able to play in any of the forward line positions, Garraty developed from a goalscorer into a schemer and in 1903 won his one and only England cap when he played against Wales. He won an FA Cup winners' medal in 1905, scoring the winning goal in Villa's 2–1 semi-final replay win over Everton at Nottingham. He had scored 111 goals in 255 league and Cup matches when, in 1908, he joined Leicester Fosse, but within a month he had signed for West Bromwich Albion before later ending his career with Lincoln City.

GEORGE, BILLY. One of the finest goalkeepers in the country, Billy George began his career with the Woolwich Ramblers in 1894 before joining the Royal Artillery the following year. Stationed at Trowbridge, Villa gave him a trial in a friendly match against West Bromwich Albion and after an impressive display, signed him. However, they had infringed FA rules and were fined £50. George, along with Fred Rinder and George Ramsay, was suspended for a month. Turning professional in October 1897, he made his debut for Villa in a 1–1 draw at the Hawthorns. Missing very few games over the next 13 seasons, he appeared in three internationals for England in 1901-02 and in 1899–1900 when Villa won the first division championship for the second year in succession, he was ever present. He played the last of his 398 first-team games in a 1–1 draw at Woolwich Arsenal in March 1911 before becoming a trainer with Birmingham City.

GERRISH, BILLY. Billy Gerrish was signed from Bristol Rovers in the summer of 1909 to partner Harry Hampton, known as the Wellington Whirlwind. But Hampton was injured and Gerrish found himself leading Villa's attack in his first few games. In fact, he scored on his debut in a 5–1 home win over Arsenal and in the club's next home game he hit a hat-trick as Villa defeated Chelsea 4–1. At the end of his first season, Gerrish had scored 14 goals in 36 league games and won a first division championship medal. Injuries plagued his career in 1910–11 and though he was fully fit for the following season, he failed to win a regular place due to the fine form of Bache, Hampton and Stephenson and the signing of Harold Halse. He left Villa and played for both Preston North End and Chesterfield. He was killed in action whilst serving with the Footballers' Battalion Middlesex Regiment in France in 1916.

GIBSON, COLIN. Joining Villa in the summer of 1976, left-back Colin Gibson made his first-team debut in November 1978 when he came on as substitute in a 2–0 win over Bristol City. In 1980–81 when Villa won the first division title, Gibson shared the number three shirt with Gary Williams, appearing in 21 of the fixtures. He was in the Villa side that beat Barcelona to win the European Super Cup in 1982–83 but in November 1985, after playing in 237 first-team games for the club he joined Manchester United for £275,000. He went straight into

Colin Gibson

71

the side at left-back but later switched to midfield. He had played in 95 games for the Reds when he joined Leicester City for £100,000 in December 1990, after a short spell on loan at Port Vale.

GIBSON, COLIN H. It was former Villa goalkeeper Cyril Spiers, then manager of Cardiff City, who introduced Colin Gibson to league football. A great favourite with the Bluebirds fans, the speedy winger played in 71 league games before he was transferred to first division Newcastle United for £15,000. He had played only 23 games for the Magpies when Villa manager Alex Massie brought him to Villa Park in February 1949 for £17,000. Making his debut in a 1–0 win at Huddersfield Town, he ended the season being chosen for the FA party to tour Scandinavia, after playing for England 'B' against Holland earlier in the campaign. His stay at Villa Park lasted seven years, in which time he scored 26 goals in 167 first-team appearances before he joined Lincoln City in January 1956 for £6,000.

GIBSON, JIMMY. Son of Neil Gibson, the former Rangers, Partick Thistle and Scottish international, Jimmy Gibson joined Villa from the Firs Park club for a then record fee of £7,500 in April 1927. A tall, commanding half-back, he had scored 43 goals in 171 league games for Thistle. He made his Villa debut in the final game of the 1926–27 season at Huddersfield and apart from the 1928–29 campaign when he suffered a serious injury, he was a regular in the Villa side for nine seasons. He represented the Scottish League and won eight full caps for Scotland, four of them while with Villa. Part of the Gibson, Talbot, Tate half-back line which served the club so well, he played the last of his 225 games for Villa in a 2–2 draw at Wolverhampton Wanderers in April 1936.

GIDMAN, JOHN. An attacking full-back famous for his fearsome tackling, John Gidman joined Aston Villa after being discarded by Liverpool. An important member of Villa's FA Youth Cup winning team of 1972, he enjoyed eight successful seasons with the club, winning one England cap and a League Cup winners' tankard in 1977. After scoring nine goals in 242 appearances, he moved back to Merseyside to join Everton, who paid a club record fee of £650,000 in October 1979 to secure his services. Gidman spent less than two years at Goodison Park, leaving in the summer of 1981 to join Manchester United. After four injury-plagued years at Old Trafford, he established himself as a first-team regular and won an FA Cup winners' medal when United beat his former club Everton in the final. Halfway through the 1986–87 season, Gidman joined Manchester City but could not prevent them from being relegated to the second division. He later joined Stoke City, where he was forced to retire because of injury in 1990.

John Gidman

GOALKEEPERS. Aston Villa FC has almost always been extremely well served by its goalkeepers and most of them have been highly popular with the supporters. Jimmy Warner was the club's first goalkeeper in the Football League. After missing just one game in each of Villa's first two seasons in the league, he was ever present in 1891–92 but when they lost 3–0 to West Bromwich Albion in that season's FA Cup final, he was held responsible for the defeat by a number of fans and had the windows of his Spring Hill pub broken. Billy George was one of the best goalkeepers in the country and as Villa's custodian, he won two first division championship medals during 398 league and Cup games for the club. Another great Villa keeper was Sam Hardy. Signed from Liverpool, Hardy was capped 21 times by England and his perfect positional sense made him the outstanding member of a Villa side that finished his first two seasons at the club as runners-up in the first division. Fred Biddlestone, signed from Walsall after he had given a great display in the Saddlers' FA Cup match with Villa, injured himself during a pre-match kick-in against Manchester City in November 1931. His replacement was Harry Morton, whom Villa had signed from the Armed Forces. Morton had conceded seven goals earlier that month when Villa beat the Army 7–0, but it didn't deter the club from signing him. One of Villa's biggest goalkeepers was Nigel Sims, standing over 6ft tall and weighing 14st. He played in 309 first-team games. When Nigel Spink came on for the injured Jimmy Rimmer during the 1982 European Cup final, it was only his second senior game for Villa. Spink went on to play in 460 first-team games for the club and became an England international when he came on as a substitute goalkeeper during the 1982–83 tour of Australasia. Villa's current goalkeeper, Mark Bosnich is an Australian international. The club paid up the remaining six months of his contract with Sydney Croatia and he has not let them down. One of the Premiership's top keepers, he has now played in well over 150 games for Villa.

GOALS. The most goals Aston Villa have scored in one match came in their 13–0 victory over Wednesbury Old Athletic in the first round of the FA Cup on 3 October 1886 at Wellington Road, Perry Barr. Dennis Hodgetts, Archie Hunter and Albert Brown all scored hat-tricks, with Loach 2, Davis and Burton scoring Villa's other goals. In the league, Villa beat Accrington 12–2 in 1891–92 and Charlton Athletic 11–1 in 1959–60.

GOALS – CAREER BEST. The highest goalscorer in the club's history is Billy Walker who between season 1919–20 and the end of season 1933–34 netted 224 goals for the club, 214 in the league and 30 in the FA Cup.

GOALS – INDIVIDUAL. Five players have scored five goals in a game for Aston Villa. The first was Harry Hampton who netted five of the goals in Villa's 10–0 win over Sheffield Wednesday on 5 October 1912. Two weeks later, Harold Halse scored all five as Villa beat Derby County 5–1 at Villa Park. Len Capewell scored five as Villa beat Burnley 10–0 on the opening day of the 1925–26 season. Six seasons later, George Brown netted five in Villa's 8–3 win at Leicester City, whilst the last player to achieve the feat was Gerry Hitchens, who scored five of Villa's goals in an 11–1 win over Charlton Athletic on 18 November 1959.

GOALS – SEASON. The club's highest league goalscorer in any one season remains Tom 'Pongo' Waring who scored 49 league goals as Villa finished second in the first division in 1930–31. He began the season in superb style, scoring all Villa's goals in a 4-3 win over Manchester United at Old Trafford on the opening day of the season. He also scored four against West Ham United (home 6–1) and Sunderland (home 4–2) and a hat-trick in a 4–1 defeat of Blackpool at Villa Park. In the final game of the season at Hillsborough, Waring needed just one more to give him 50 league goals but he hit the woodwork twice and further efforts were brilliantly saved by the Owls' keeper Breedon. Waring did score in Villa's 3–1 FA Cup defeat at home to Arsenal, so did in fact score 50 goals that season.

GOALSCORING RECORDS. Aston Villa scored 128 goals in 42 division one matches during the 1930-31 season. They scored in every home match (86 goals) and failed in only three away. In 20 home games, four goals or more were recorded. At Villa Park, Middlesbrough were beaten 8–1, Manchester United 7–0, Huddersfield Town 6–1 and Arsenal 5–1. Villa also won 6–1 at Huddersfield and 4–0 at Birmingham. Top scorer was Tom 'Pongo' Waring with 49 goals, while Eric Houghton had 30. Yet Villa could only finish as runners-up to Arsenal. Aston Villa became the first club to score 6,000 league goals on 17 October 1987 when Mark Walters scored in the 1–1 draw against Bournemouth.

GODFREY, BRIAN. Following trials with Wrexham, Chester and Tranmere Rovers, Brian Godfrey played for Flint Alexandra before signing professional forms for Everton. After just one game for the Toffees, he moved to Scunthorpe United where he netted 24 goals in 87 outings. In October 1963 he transferred to Preston North End and in four seasons, scored 52 goals in 122 appearances. His best season was 1964–65 when he scored 25 goals in 37 league games. The following season, he scored the club's fastest-ever hat-trick when he hit three goals in five minutes in North End's 9–0 drubbing of Cardiff City. He joined Villa in September 1967, scoring on his debut in a 1–1 draw at Middlesbrough. In fact, he scored in each of his first three games for the club, ending the season with 13 goals in 35 league and Cup appearances. A Welsh international, he was exchanged for Bristol

Rovers' Ray Graydon in the summer of 1971, scoring 18 goals in 90 appearances during his time at Eastville. He later played for Newport County before entering management, first with Exeter City and then with non-league Bath City, Weymouth and Gloucester City in 1992.

GOFFIN, BILLY. After playing his early football with Tamworth in the Birmingham Combination League, Billy Goffin signed professional forms for Aston Villa in December 1937, yet had to wait nine years for his league debut. He played in 87 games for Villa during the war years, scoring 50 goals, including four in the 19–2 win over RAF Lichfield in a Birmingham and District League game. A fast, direct winger, Goffin was nicknamed Cowboy and thrilled the crowds with his touchline play. He appeared in 173 league and Cup games for Villa before ending his League career with Walsall. He returned to Tamworth and had a short spell as manager before leaving the game for good in 1958.

GRAY, ANDY. One of the bravest strikers of his generation, Andy Gray joined Aston Villa from Dundee United for £110,000 in September 1975, after scoring 44 goals in 76 games for the Tannadice club. In 1976–77 when Villa finished fourth in the first division and won the League Cup, Gray was the club's top scorer with 29 goals in 48 appearances. He was voted PFA Player of the Year and Young Player of the Year. His stay at Villa Park lasted four years. In September 1979, he moved to Wolverhampton Wanderers for a British record fee of £1.5 million. Four years later he moved again, this

Andy Gray

time to Everton for £250,000. He scored the second goal in the Toffees' 1984 FA Cup final win and the first in the 1985 European Cup-Winners' Cup triumph. At the end of that season, aged 29, he was dramatically recalled into the Scotland side, eventually ending with 20 full caps to his name. In 1985, he rejoined Villa for £150,000 but after a loan spell with Notts County, he signed for West Bromwich Albion in 1987. In his two spells with the club, he had appeared in 210 first-team games, scoring 78 goals. He retired from football shortly after his arrival at the Hawthorns and in the summer of 1991 returned to Villa Park for a third time as assistant manager to Ron Atkinson. He resigned in 1992 to pursue a career in television with Sky.

GRAY, STUART. Stuart Gray started his career with Nottingham Forest but in March 1983 despite having missed only a handful of games since his debut against Manchester City in February 1981, he went on loan to Bolton Wanderers. That summer he left the City Ground and joined Barnsley, where he played in 136 first-team games before his transfer to Aston Villa in November 1987 for £150,000. He quickly fitted into the Villa midfield and scored five valuable goals in 19 appearances as the club won promotion to the first division as runners-up. He later moved to left-back but after playing in 132 games for the club, he was allowed to join Southampton for £200,000. Unfortunately, an Achilles tendon injury reduced his first-team appearances and eventually forced his retirement from the game.

GRAYDON, RAY. Ray Graydon joined his home-town club, Bristol Rovers, on leaving school in 1963, and in six seasons at Eastville club, scored 33 goals in 133 league appearances. He signed for Villa in the summer of 1971 with Brian Godfrey going in the opposite direction. In his first season with the club, he played in every game bar one, finishing as second top scorer with 14 goals as Villa won the third division championship. In 1975, Graydon scored the winning goal for Villa in the League Cup final at Wembley after Norwich City goalkeeper Kevin Keelan palmed his penalty on to the post and the ball rebounded back into play for him to smash into an empty net. He won a second League Cup winners' medal in 1977 after Villa had beaten Everton over three games but in the close season he joined Coventry City. After just one season at Highfield Road, he went to play for the Washington Diplomats in the NASL before returning to these shores to play for Oxford United, later becoming coach at the Manor Ground.

GRIFFITHS, TOM. Welsh international centre-half Tom Griffiths began his career with his home-town club Wrexham in 1922 before joining Everton seven years later. After 78 games for the Goodison Park club, he had spells with Bolton Wanderers and Middlesbrough before signing for Villa in November 1935. Despite his efforts in his first season with the club, Villa were relegated to the second division, a fate he had suffered with Everton and Bolton Wanderers in seasons 1929–30 and 1932–33. He was capped by Wales on 21 occasions, four of his caps being won whilst with Villa. He had played in 67 first-team matches for the club when illness forced his retirement from the game.

GROVES, WILLIE. One of the club's earliest utility players, Willie Groves played in four different positions in his one season with Villa. Throughout his career, he played in nine outfield positions. Born in Leith, he joined Hibernian in 1887 from the Thistle Club of Edinburgh and in that season won a Scottish Cup winners' medal. He spent a season with Celtic before coming south to play for West Bromwich Albion. A Scottish international, he scored four goals on his second appearance against Ireland. He played in 67 games for Albion before joining Villa in the summer of 1893. He scored three goals in 26 league and Cup appearances before returning to Hibernian at the end of the 1893-94 season.

GUEST PLAYERS. The guest system was used by all clubs during the two wars. Although at times it was abused almost beyond belief (some sides that opposed Villa had ten or even 11 guests!) it normally worked sensibly and effectively to the benefit of players, clubs and supporters alike. A number of Villa players guested for other clubs during the Second World War and these included Jimmy Allen for Birmingham City, Fulham and Portsmouth; George Cummings for Birmingham City, Falkirk, Northampton Town and Nottingham Forest; George Edwards for Birmingham City, Coventry City, Northampton Town, Nottingham Forest, Notts County and West Bromwich Albion; Bob Iverson for Birmingham City, Northampton Town, Nottingham Forest and

Notts County; Albert Kerr for Charlton Athletic, Luton Town, Northampton Town, Plymouth Argyle and Portsmouth; Frank Moss junior for Birmingham City and Northampton Town and Joe Rutherford for Nottingham Forest.

H

HALL, ALBERT. Signed from Stourbridge in 1903, Albert Hall scored six goals in his nine league outings during 1903-04, including one on his debut in a 7-3 win at Nottingham Forest. A hard-working outside-left, Hall teamed up well with Joe Bache and over the next six seasons, the two of them terrorised opposition defences. With Villa, Hall won an FA Cup winners' medal in 1905 and a first division championship medal in 1910, the year he won his only England cap when he played against Ireland. A consistent goalscorer, he netted 61 in 214 league and Cup appearances but lost out to Bache in Villa's FA Cup final side of 1913, as his former left-wing partner moved outside to accommodate Clem Stephenson. Later that year, Hall joined Millwall Athletic before retiring in 1916.

HALSE, HAROLD. Though he only spent one season with Aston Villa, Harold Halse was the club's top scorer with 28 goals in 37 appearances and won an FA Cup winners' medal after Sunderland were beaten 1–0 in the final. Manchester United signed him from Southend United in March 1908 to partner Sandy Turnbull in the Old Trafford club's forward line. He won an FA Cup winners' medal with United in 1909, the year that he won his only England cap, scoring twice in an 8–1 win over Austria in Vienna. In the FA Charity Shield match of 1911, Halse scored a hat-trick in each half of a match that saw United beat Swindon Town 8–4. He scored 50 goals for United before signing for Aston Villa in the summer of 1912. In only his ninth match for the Villans, he scored all five goals in a 5–1 win over Derby County, to equal Harry Hampton's club record for most goals in a game. At the end of the 1912–13 season, he joined Chelsea, where he continued to be a prolific goalscorer, before ending his career with Charlton Athletic.

HAMILTON, IAN. Ian 'Chico' Hamilton made his league debut for Chelsea against Tottenham Hotspur when he was just 16 years old. An England youth international, he moved to Southend United in September 1968 before transferring to Aston Villa for £40,000 in the summer of 1969. After making 17 appearances in his first season at Villa Park, he won a regular place in 1970–71 and picked up a League Cup runners-up medal after Villa had been beaten 2–0 by Tottenham Hotspur in the final. The following season he played an important role in helping Villa win the third division championship and in 1975 collected a League Cup winners' medal after Norwich City had been beaten 1–0. He played the last of his 249 first-team games for Villa in a 3–2 defeat at Birmingham City in April 1976. That summer he signed for Sheffield United and played in 60 league games for the Bramall Lane club before ending his career playing in the NASL.

HAMPTON, HARRY. Known as the Wellington Whirlwind, Harry Hampton scored 54 goals in two seasons for his home-town club, before joining Aston Villa in May 1904. He stayed with the club until February 1920, scoring 242 goals in 373 league and Cup matches. His total of 215 league goals remains the club record. He scored 14 hat-tricks including five goals when Villa beat Sheffield Wednesday 10–0 on 5 October 1912 and both goals when they won the FA Cup in 1905, beating Newcastle United 2–0. He won another FA Cup winners' medal in 1913 and a league championship medal in 1909–10, when he topped the club goalscoring charts with 26 goals in 32 league matches. He was capped four times by England, winning his first against Scotland in 1913. Hampton owed many of his goals to the fine crosses of Brawn, Hall and Wallace, and made his name by charging the opposition goalkeeper, many of whom ended up in the back of the net with the ball. He played his last game for Villa in a 2–2 draw at home to Burnley on 3 January 1920, before leaving to play for neighbours and rivals, Birmingham. He helped the Blues win the second division title in 1921, later playing for Newport County and Wellington. He ended his involvement with the game after a spell as coach at Preston North End.

HARDY, SAM. One of the greatest goalkeepers of all-time, Sam Hardy began his professional career with Chesterfield from whom Liverpool signed him in October 1905. At Anfield, he won 14 England caps and appeared in 239 first-team games before transferring to Aston Villa in the summer of 1912. He made his debut in the opening game of the following season, keeping a clean sheet as Villa beat Chelsea 1–0. At the end of his first season at Villa Park, he won an FA Cup winners' medal as Villa beat Sunderland 1–0 at Crystal Palace. In fact, in the six Cup matches that season, Hardy only conceded one goal and that was in the 3–1 first-round win at Derby County. Also that season, he gained the first of another seven caps he was to win with England, starring in the 1–0 win over Scotland at Stamford Bridge. During the First World War, he served in the Royal Navy. He guested for Nottingham Forest when they won the Victory Shield in 1919, but returned to Villa and in 1920 won his second FA Cup winners' medal. He had played in 183 first-team games for Villa when in August 1921 he was allowed to join Nottingham Forest on a permanent basis. During his first season at the City Ground, he helped them win the second division title. He had to retire from the game in October 1924 at the age of 41, following an injury sustained against Newcastle United.

HARROP, JIMMY. After playing as an amateur for Sheffield Wednesday, Jimmy Harrop turned professional with Rotherham Town before signing for Liverpool. Succeeding Alex Raisbeck, Harrop played in 139 league and Cup games for the Anfield side before transferring to Aston Villa in May 1912. He won an FA Cup winners' medal the following season when Villa beat Sunderland 1–0 and though he played in all the earlier round matches, he missed the semi-final and final of 1920 through injury. A great success at Villa Park, Harrop missed very few games in his five seasons with the club and though he never played for England, he appeared for the Football League and had trials for his country. He ended his career with Sheffield United.

HATELEY, TONY. One of the game's top marksmen, Tony Hateley began his career with Notts County where he scored 77 goals in 131 league appearances before signing for Villa in the summer of 1963. He made his debut on the opening day of the 1963–64 season, scoring the only goal of the game in Villa's 1–0 win at Nottingham Forest. The following season, he was an ever-present and the club's leading scorer with 20 League goals. He also scored 14 Cup goals, including four in the 7–1 win over Bradford City in the fifth round of the League Cup. In 1965–66, he had his best league season for the Villans, scoring 27 goals in 39 appearances, including four in the 5–5 draw against Spurs at White Hart Lane. After scoring 86 goals in 148 first-team appearances, he joined Chelsea for £100,000, gaining an FA Cup runners-up medal with the Stamford Bridge club in 1967. At the end of that season, he moved to Liverpool for another £100,000 and after joining Coventry City in September 1968, he played for Birmingham City before returning to Notts County. Hateley ended his league career with Oldham Athletic, having scored 211 goals in 434 league appearances with his seven clubs.

HAT-TRICK HEROES. Albert Allen scored Aston Villa's first Football League hat-trick on 29 September 1888 when Notts County were beaten 9–1. Allen also marked his England debut with a hat-trick in a 5–1 win over Ireland in Belfast in March of that year but, unbelievably, it was his only international appearance. A number of other Villa players marked their international debut with hat-tricks. When England beat Ireland 13–0 in Belfast on 18 February 1882, Howard Vaughton scored five and Arthur Brown three; in 1897, Fred Wheldon scored three goals as England beat Ireland 6–0 at Nottingham. No one has scored three goals on their debut, but Billy Walker scored a hat-trick of penalties for Villa in their 7–1 defeat of Bradford City at Villa Park on 12 November 1921. Stan Lynn hit a hat-trick against Sunderland in January 1958 as Villa won 5–2. Lynn was the first full-back in the first division to score a hat-trick. Central defender Allan Evans scored a double hat-trick in a Central League game against Sheffield United in February 1978 after he had been asked to play up front. The most hat-tricks scored for the club is 14 by Harry Hampton, one of Villa's greatest-ever forwards.

HAYCOCK, FREDDIE. Liverpool-born Haycock began his footballing career with Bootle Boys, but on leaving school he went to work in his family's butchery business. After visiting Ireland for his summer holidays, he was asked to play for Waterford and a good number of years later was selected for an Irish representative team despite being English. He was playing inside-right for Prescot Cables when Villa signed him in 1934, though he had to wait for the reshuffle at the club before making his debut in the 3–0 win over Norwich City in December 1936. He played in 110 league and Cup games for Villa before the war and then scored 24 goals in 84 wartime appearances for the club as well as guesting for Notts County, Nottingham Forest, Northampton, Plymouth and Wolves. In 1946, he joined Wrexham but only had one season at the Racecourse Ground before retiring.

HEADERS. Aston Villa players scored the two longest distance headed goals in Football League games. Frank Barson scored with a header from 30 yards against Sheffield United on Boxing Day 1921 to give Villa a 3–2 victory; and Peter Aldis achieved his feat from 35 yards against Sunderland on 1 September 1952 as Villa won 3-0.

HITCHENS, GERRY. Gerry Hitchens began his Football League career with Cardiff City when he joined them from Kidderminster Harriers in 1953. At Ninian Park, he scored 40 goals in 95 league games before signing for Villa for £22,500 in December 1957. He made his debut for Villa in a disastrous 2–0 home defeat by Birmingham City, but scored three goals in his next two games to give notice of his goalscoring ability. His first hat-trick for the club came the following season when he hit all three goals in a 3–1 win at Bolton Wanderers. During the 1959–60 season, Hitchens scored ten goals in three successive games, including five in the 11–1 thrashing of Charlton Athletic which equalled the club record for the most goals scored by one player in a league game. That season he topped the club's goalscoring charts with 23 league goals as they won the second division championship. In 1960–61 he achieved the feat again, this time with 29 goals. He also helped Villa to the League Cup final, scoring in every round of the competition. Despite those 11 goals he missed the final against Rotherham United because it had been put back to the start of the following season and by that time he had joined Italian giants Inter Milan. A most popular player, the England international stayed in Italy for eight years, playing for Torino, Atalanta and Cagliari after his days at Inter were over. He returned to England in 1969 to play for Worcester City and retired after a short spell with Merthyr Tydfil. Voted Midlands Player of the Year in 1961, Hitchens scored 96 goals in 160 games for the Villa Park club.

HODGE, STEVE. Figuring prominently in Brian Clough's plans, Steve Hodge missed only a handful of games in three seasons in the Nottingham Forest first team. Just two games into the 1985–86 season, he was rather surprisingly allowed to join Aston Villa for £450,000. He impressed immediately at Villa Park, enough to warrant a full England cap when he replaced Gordon Cowans during a 1–0 win over Russia in March 1986. After he had played in five games in the 1986 World Cup, another large fee

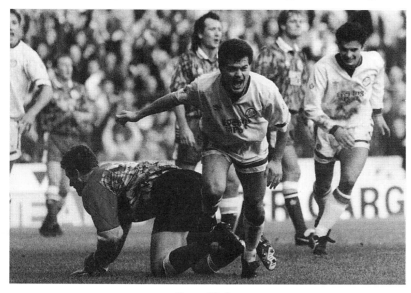

Steve Hodge

changed hands as he joined Tottenham Hotspur. He failed to settle at White Hart Lane and returned to the City Ground for a second spell with Forest. He won two League Cup winners' medals and came on as substitute when Forest lost to Spurs in the FA Cup final of 1991, but he was frequently plagued by injuries and in July of that year he was allowed to join Leeds United. He later went to Derby County on loan before signing for Queens Park Rangers.

HODGETTS, DENNIS. England winger Dennis Hodgetts joined Villa from Birmingham St George in February 1886. In his first FA Cup game for the club, the 13–0 win over Wednesbury Old Athletic, he scored a hat-trick. At the end of his first season he had an FA Cup winners' medal. In fact, Hodgetts scored the first goal for Villa in their 2–0 win over West Bromwich Albion at Kennington Oval. He won another FA Cup winners' medal in 1895 and on either side of that year, won a league championship medal. Quite a prolific scorer for a winger, his best season was that of 1893–94 when he scored 12 League goals in 29 appearances. Possessing a powerful shot, many of his goals were scored from distance and in 218 league and Cup games for the club, he scored 91 goals. He left Villa in 1896 to join Small Heath, missing out on the club's double-winning season.

HODGSON, GORDON. Born in Johannesburg, Gordon Hodgson was persuaded to join Liverpool after he had impressed for Transvaal during Liverpool's tour of the country in 1924–25. In 11 seasons for the Anfield club, he scored 240 goals in 378 league and Cup matches. In 1930–31, he scored a record 37 league goals, including four hat-tricks and a four against Sheffield Wednesday at Hillsborough. Also that season he was capped three times by England, having represented the Football League on two occasions. A good all-round sportsman, he played cricket for Lancashire and Transvaal, taking 148 wickets at 27.75 runs apiece for the Red Rose county. He joined Villa in January 1936 and made his debut at Deepdale against Preston North End later that month. Though he stayed at Villa Park for only 14 months, he scored 11 goals in 28 appearances including a hat-trick in a 5–1 win over Bradford City on 14 September 1936. He moved to Leeds United in March 1937, later becoming coach at Elland

Road before taking over as Port Vale manager, a position he held for five years until his death at the age of 47.

HOGAN, JIMMY. An average player, Jimmy Hogan won two Scottish league championship medals and appeared in an FA Cup semi-final with Fulham before going to coach in Holland. Two years later, he went to Austria where he formed a famous partnership with Hugo Meisl. These two were given much of the credit for the development of the game in Europe. In 1934, Hogan returned to England to manage Fulham, but the players and directors did not like his training methods and tactics and he was relieved of his duties whilst in hospital recovering from illness. After a short spell in Austria again, where he helped the national side to the 1936 Olympic Football final, he returned to England to take charge of Aston Villa in November 1936. He led Villa to promotion from the second division in his second season and to an FA Cup semi-final in 1938. The Second World War ended his connection with the club although after the hostilities, Villa were one of three clubs to benefit from his development of the youth scheme. Later he went to coach in Hungary and inspired the great Puskas–Hidegkuti Hungarian side that beat England 6–3 at Wembley in 1953.

HOLTE END. The Holte End was named after Sir Thomas Holte, resident of nearby Aston Hall in the 17th century. It was extended in 1939, and in 1990 its facilities were upgraded and its roof extended in preparation for the 1994 all-seater deadline. On 7 May 1994 came the Holte End's final hour as 19,210 Villa fans packed in to see Liverpool beaten 2–1. Each one of those Villa fans was handed a certificate on which the words 'I was there' were printed. Within eight months, the largest end terrace in the Football League was replaced by the largest end stand, housing 13,462 seats at a cost of £5.3 million.

HOME MATCHES. Villa's best home wins are the 13–0 victory over Wednesbury Old Athletic in a first-round FA Cup match on 30 October 1886 and the 13–1 win against the Casuals, also in a first round FA Cup match on 17 January 1891. Dennis Hodgetts scored hat-tricks in both of those matches. Villa's biggest league victory at home is the 12–2 win over Accrington on 12 March

1892. Villa's worst home defeat is 7–0, a scoreline inflicted upon them by West Bromwich Albion on 19 October 1935 in a season in which they conceded seven goals at home in three matches. Villa have scored double figures at home in four other matches: King's Lynn 11–0 (FA Cup 1905–06); Sheffield Wednesday 10–0 (division one 1912–13); Burnley 10–0 (division one 1925–26) and Charlton Athletic 11–1 (division two 1959–60).

HOME SEASONS. Aston Villa have gone through a complete league season with an undefeated home record on three occasions: 1895–96, 1898–99 and 1909–10. The club's highest number of home wins in a league season is 20. This was achieved in 1971–72 from 23 matches as they won the third division championship.

HONOURS. The major honours achieved by the club are:

First division championship	1893–94
	1895–96
	1896–97
	1898–99
	1899–00
	1909–10
	1980–81
Second division championship	1937–38
	1959–60
Third division championship	1971–72
FA Cup	1887
	1895
	1897
	1913
	1920
	1957
Football League Cup	1961
	1975
	1977
	1994
	1996
FA Charity Shield	1981 (shared)
European Cup	1981–82
European Super Cup	1983

HOUGHTON, ERIC. One of the greatest names in Aston Villa's history, Eric Houghton was born in Billingborough, Lincolnshire, on 19 June 1910. After leaving Donnington School, he played as a utility forward for Boston Town and Billingborough before joining Aston Villa as an amateur in August 1927, turning professional twelve months later. He graduated through the club's junior and reserve sides to make his first-team debut against Leeds United in January 1930. Villa lost the game 4–3 in front of a 32,476 crowd. Lining up at outside-left, he was to make the position his own over the next 16 years or so. He scored twice in a 5–1 FA Cup win over Reading a week after making his debut. He went on to score 170 goals in 392 appearances in major league and Cup competitions. During the war, he was also a prominent member of Villa's first XI and between 1939 and 1946 he netted 87 goals in 158 matches, helping Villa win the Football League (North) Cup in 1944. Eric was a penalty expert. He put his full weight into his spot-kicks, smashing the ball as hard as he could towards goal. His success rate was second to none – over 60 penalties converted out of 70 taken. He had one of the game's hardest shots and twice sent the ball straight through the back of the net when scoring for Villa. He won seven caps for England and was on the winning side in six of those matches; England scored 28 goals with Houghton claiming five. He left Villa Park just after the war and joined Notts County before returning to take charge of his beloved Aston Villa in 1953. Four years later he proudly saw his team win the FA Cup for the first time since 1920 but sadly after a series of poor results, he was sacked in November 1958 and succeeded by Joe Mercer.

HOUGHTON, RAY. An industrious midfield player, Ray Houghton made his league debut for West Ham United, coming on as a substitute at Arsenal in May 1982. That was the only chance he got at Upton Park and on being freed joined Fulham. After 145 league and Cup games for the Cottagers, he signed for Oxford United, newly promoted to the first division. In his first season at the Manor Ground, he scored the second goal in a 3–0 League Cup final win over Queens Park Rangers and won the first of 64 caps for the Republic of Ireland. Signed by Liverpool in October 1987, he went on to win a league championship medal in

Ray Houghton

his first season. The following term he played in every game, picking up an FA Cup winners' medal. During the summer of 1992, he joined Aston Villa for a fee of £900,000 and the following season they did the league double over his former team. He made 121 first-team appearances for Villa before lending his experience to Crystal Palace, where he went in March 1995 for £300,000.

HUNDRED GOALS. Aston Villa have scored more than 100 league goals in a season on two occasions. The highest total is 128 goals, scored in 1930–31 when they finished the season as runners-up to Arsenal in the first division. Villa scored 104 goals the following season when finishing fifth. Villa have conceded more than 100 goals in a season on only one occasion and that was in 1935–36 when they let in 110 goals and were relegated to the second division.

HUNT, STEVE. Born at Witton, midfielder Steve Hunt made his Villa debut at Sheffield Wednesday, coming on as a substitute for Ian Hamilton in a 4–0 win. Unable to break into the Villa first team on a regular basis, he left the club and English football, signing for New York Cosmos in the NASL for £50,000. He helped Cosmos win the NASL Championships in 1977 and again in 1978, but in September of that year, he returned to these shores, signing for Coventry City, where he played in 185 league games before joining West Bromwich Albion in March 1984 for £80,000. He won two caps for England whilst with the Baggies but when former Villa boss Ron Saunders arrived to manage the Albion, Hunt's face did not fit and he rejoined Villa in a deal involving Darren Bradley plus £90,000. After appearing in the last 12 games of the 1985–86 season, he was one of the few Villa players to come out of the following season's relegation to the second division with any credit. After Graham Taylor was appointed Villa boss in July 1987, Hunt's appearances were restricted and in November of that year, injury forced his retirement from the game.

HUNTER, ARCHIE. One of the club's greatest-ever captains, Archie Hunter was the first Villa skipper to lift the FA Cup, when they beat West Bromwich Albion 2–0 at Kennington Oval. During that season, the Ayrshire-born player scored in every round of the FA Cup, including a hat-trick in the 13–0 first-round win over Wednesbury Old Athletic and the second goal in the final itself. He had joined Villa in 1879 after a business engagement brought him to the Midlands. He was attempting to locate the Calthorpe Club which toured the Ayrshire coast where he used to live, but inadvertently fate led him to Villa, where he stayed. In fact, in his early days with the club, Hunter had to play under an assumed name as one of his employers hated football and would most certainly have sacked him if he had known he was playing for Villa. The Villa captain's career came to a most tragic end. He was playing at centre-forward for the club against Everton at Anfield on 4 January 1890 when he suffered a heart attack. He was taken to hospital but never really recovered and died in November 1894, aged 35.

I

INJURIES. The risk of injury is an ever-present threat in the game of football and all professional players expect to miss some games through injury at some point in their careers. Villa's Albert Evans broke his leg three times whilst with the club, once when he was attempting to clear a ditch in training. In fact, the unlucky Evans broke his leg on a further two occasions, one being on Christmas Day 1908 when he was captaining West Bromwich Albion, whom he had joined two years earlier, and the other after he had hung up his boots and was turning out in a charity game in 1915. Harold Edgley broke his leg in the 2–1 defeat at Chelsea just three weeks before Villa played on the same Stamford Bridge ground in the FA Cup final of 1920 against Huddersfield Town. Edgley had scored against Chelsea in the semi-final and played in every round of that season's competition, so the club presented him with a special souvenir medal after Villa had won 1–0. Joining Villa from Norwich City in the summer of 1938, George Cummings chipped a bone in his ankle after being tackled by Bob Iverson during training and had to delay his debut for two months. John Gidman suffered a serious eye injury in November 1974 when a firework exploded in his face. He was out of the game for five months and missed the League Cup final of 1975.

INTERNATIONAL MATCHES. Villa Park has been host to

seven full international matches involving England. The first was on 25 February 1893 when England beat Ireland 6–1. England met Scotland for the first time at Villa Park on 8 April 1899 and, with Villa's Jimmy Crabtree and Charlie Athersmith in their ranks, won 2–1. The two sides met again on 3 May 1900 and drew 2–2. England had Billy George and Albert Wilkes in their side. The last time England entertained Scotland at Villa Park was on 8 April 1922. Despite having three Villa players on duty – Frank Moss, Dick York and Billy Walker – they lost 1-0 to give the visitors their first victory on English soil since 1893. The biggest crowd for an international match at Villa Park, 67,770, saw England defeat Wales 1–0 on 10 November 1948. In the sixth international match, played on 14 November 1951, Bolton's Nat Lofthouse scored both goals in a 2–0 win over Northern Ireland. The final international match involving England to be played at Villa Park was on 26 November 1958 against Wales when Wolverhampton Wanderers' Peter Broadbent netted both England goals in a 2–2 draw. A Victory International was played at Villa Park in February 1945 when England beat Scotland 3–2. In 1966, three World Cup group matches were played there, whilst in 1996, three European Championship group matches were played at Villa Park along with a quarter-final match between Czechoslovakia and Portugal.

INTERNATIONAL PLAYERS. Villa's most capped player i.e. caps gained while players were registered with the club, is Paul McGrath with 51 caps. The following is a complete list of players who have gained full international honours while at Villa Park.

England		Scotland	
A. Allen	1	D. Blair	1
C.W. Athersmith	12	J.Cowan	3
J.W. Bache	7	G. Cummings	6
F. Barson	1	A. Evans	4
J. Beresford	1	J. Gibson	4
G.F. Blackburn	1	A.Gray	6
W.F. Brawn	2	A. McInally	2
F.H. Broome	7	A. Massie	7
A. Brown	3	T.B. Niblo	1
G. Brown	1	R. Templeton	1
G. Cowans	8		

J.W. Crabtree	11	*Northern Ireland*	
A. Daley	4	R.D. Blanchflower	8
J.H.G. Devey	2	A.D. Dougan	3
A.R. Dorrell	4	N. Lockhart	4
A. Ducat	3	P.J. McParland	33
U. Ehiogu	1	C.J. Martin	2
T. Gardner	2	S.J. Morgan	8
W. Garraty	1	C.J. Nicholl	12
W. George	3	W.T. Renneville	1
J. Gidman	1	*Wales*	
A.E. Hall	1	D.J. Astley	9
H. Hampton	4	V.H. Crowe	16
S. Hardy	7	R.E. Evans	4
G. Hitchens	3	W.G. Evans	1
S.B. Hodge	8	T. Ford	14
D. Hodgetts	6	A.W. Green	1
W.E. Houghton	7	T.P. Griffiths	4
W.J. Kirton	1	T. Hockey	1
A. Leake	5	B. Hole	4
B. Little	1	K. Jones	1
E. Lowe	3	C. Phillips	3
A.W. Morley	6	L. Phillips	26
T. Mort	3	I.V. Powell	4
F. Moss Snr	5	H. Price	1
B. Olney	2	D. Saunders	14
D. Platt	22	A.E. Watkins	2
J. Reynolds	5	W.M.Watkins	3
T. Smart	1	A.P. Woosnam	2
S. Smith	1		
G.Southgate	9	*Republic of Ireland*	
H. Spencer	6	A. Cascarino	15
N. Spink	1	E. Deacy	4
R. Starling	1	T. Donovan	1
J.T. Tate	3	G. Farrelly	3
T. Thompson	1	A. Hale	1
H.A. Vaughton	5	P. McGrath	51
W.H. Walker	18	C.J. Martin	24
C.W. Wallace	3	T. Muldoon	1
T. Waring	5	P. Saward	13
O. Whateley	2	S. Staunton	36

G.F. Wheldon	4	A. Townsend	21
A. Wilkes	5	D.J. Walsh	6
P. Withe	11		
R.E. York	2		

Villa's first player to be capped was Howard Vaughton who played for England against Ireland on 18 February 1881. Villa have also had a number of foreign internationals on their books. They include current players Mark Bosnich (Australia) and Dwight Yorke (Trinidad and Tobago), along with former players Kent Nielsen (Denmark), Didier Six (France) and Dariusz Kubicki (Poland).

IVERSON, BOB. After playing his early football with Folkestone Town, Bob Iverson joined Tottenham Hotspur in 1932, playing in the club's nursery side, Northfleet, before leaving to play for Ramsgate. His first taste of league football came with Lincoln City and then Wolverhampton Wanderers, before he signed for Villa in December 1936. Iverson made his debut in a 3–0 win over Norwich City and went on to be a regular member of the Villa side until 1947. On 3 December 1938, Iverson scored Villa's fastest-ever goal, less than ten seconds into the game against Charlton Athletic, which Villa won 2–0. During the war, he played in 179 games for Villa and won a League Cup (North) winners' medal, as well as

Bob Iverson

guesting for Birmingham, Northampton Town, Notts County and Nottingham Forest. He played his last game for Villa in August 1947, retiring to coach the club's reserve side.

J

JACKSON, TOMMY. Eventually succeeding Sam Hardy, goalkeeper Tommy Jackson made his Villa debut in a 1–0 win against Sunderland at Roker Park on 23 February 1921. The following season he played in the first 39 games before injury in the game against Chelsea at Villa Park caused him to miss being an ever-present. Jackson was always in competition with Cyril Spiers for the first-team goalkeeper's jersey but appeared for Villa in the 1924 FA Cup final against Newcastle United. Something of a penalty expert, he saved nine during his Villa career, Jackson left the club in 1931 after playing in 186 league and Cup games to concentrate on a career in teaching after qualifying at Durham University.

JOACHIM, JULIAN. Peterborough-born Julian Joachim is an outstanding young talent, yet to develop fully. Starting his league career with Leicester City, he won international honours at Youth and Under-21 level and scored the club's first-ever goal in the Premier League in the 3–1 home defeat by Newcastle United on the opening day of the 1994–95 season. He scored a brace of goals in the 3–1 win over Spurs but a broken foot which was not immediately diagnosed sidelined him until the last two matches. The following season, he appeared to have lost his way with the Filbert Street club and in February 1996 he joined his former manager Brian Little at Villa Park in a deal worth £1.5 million. Though he scored on his first full appearance for the club in a 2–0 win over Blackburn Rovers, he spent most of his time on the bench.

JOHNSON, GEORGE. Born in West Bromwich, George Johnson played with a number of local clubs before signing professional forms with Albion in May 1895. Having little opportunity to show his value at first-team level, he left to join Walsall before signing for Villa in August 1897. He made his league debut in the final match of that season, scoring the second goal in Villa's 2–0 win over Nottingham Forest after having spent the entire campaign playing in the reserves. In 1898–99, his first full season, he scored ten goals and collected a league championship medal. He helped Villa retain the title the following season and hit a hat-trick in a 4–1 win at Notts County. In 1900–01 he scored four goals in Villa's 7–1 win at home to Manchester City and another three in the 5–0 first round win over Millwall. Scoring 47 goals in his 108 first-team appearances, he was forced to hang up his boots in the summer of 1906 following a serious leg injury.

JOHNSON, TOMMY. Geordie Tommy Johnson began his league career with Notts County in 1989, but after appearing in 149 first-team games for the Meadow Lane club, joined Derby County for £1.3 million in March 1992. He was part of the deal that brought Gary Charles from Derby County to Villa Park in January 1995. Prior to his move to Villa, he had scored seven goals in 14 league games for the Rams, whilst overall he had netted 41 goals in 129 games. A month after he arrived at Villa Park, he hit a first-half hat-trick in the club's 7–1 thrashing of Wimbledon as Villa recorded their biggest win for 33 years. After that he picked up a hamstring injury which caused him to struggle for the rest of the campaign. Though he spent the early part of the following season on the bench, he came on as substitute at Upton Park, scoring one goal and creating another in Villa's 4–1 win. Regaining his first-team place, he adopted a policy of shoot on sight and though he scored the League Cup quarter-final winner against Wolverhampton Wanderers, he was on the bench for the final at Wembley.

JONES, KEITH. Welsh international goalkeeper Keith Jones joined Villa from Kidderminster Harriers in the summer of 1946 and was given his league debut at Molineux in December of that year. Unfortunately he did not have the best of games as Villa went down 4–1, but he held his place for the rest of the season. In 1949, he won his only international cap when he played against Scotland in Glasgow, Wales going down 2–0. After that he was hampered by injuries, lost his first-team place and asked to be placed on the transfer list, but he won his place back midway through the 1952–53 season. He played in 199 games for the club until the arrival of Nigel Sims from Wolverhampton Wanderers. After leaving Villa for Port Vale in 1957, he had spells with Crewe Alexandra and Southport before retiring.

JUBILEE FUND. The League Benevolent Fund was launched in 1938, 50 years after the start of the Football League, to benefit players who had fallen on hard times. It was decided that the best way to raise funds was for sides to play local derby games with no account being taken of league status. Villa played West Bromwich Albion at Villa Park in front of 26,640, with Frank Broome scoring their goal in a 1–1 draw. The fixture, reversed for the start of the 1939–40 season, was played at the Hawthorns. The result was the same with Eric Houghton netting for Villa.

K

KEOWN, MARTIN. After turning professional with Arsenal, Martin Keown found his chances limited and went on loan to Brighton and Hove Albion for whom he made his Football league debut. He returned to Highbury midway through the 1985–86 season and won a place at the heart of the Gunners defence. However, during the close season Villa signed him. He made his debut for the club, at Loftus Road in August, at right-back but after a handful of games in this position, he reverted to a more central role. Despite Keown playing well, the club were relegated to the second division. He was an important member of the Villa side and helped them regain their first division status at the first attempt. He had played in 133 games for the club when he joined Everton in August 1989 for £750,000. Despite the presence of Ratcliffe and Watson, Keown was firmly established at the heart of Everton's defence and in February 1992 won the first of his 11 international caps. A great favourite with the Goodison crowd, it came as a great surprise when he returned to Arsenal for £2 million in February 1993.

KERR, ALBERT. Joining Villa in the summer of 1936, Albert Kerr made his first-team debut in the 2–1 win at Swansea Town on the opening day of the 1936–37 season, though for most of that campaign he played in the reserves, helping them win the

Birmingham Combination and Mid-Week league championships. By 1938–39 he had won a regular place in the Villa side but, after injuring his hip, he lost his spot to Frank Broome. With the arrival of war, Kerr guested for a number of league clubs as well as playing in a few games for Villa. When peacetime football resumed in 1946–47 he played in only one match, against Portsmouth for whom he had guested during the hostilities, before injury ended his career.

KINGDON, BILLY. Wing-half Billy Kingdon joined Villa from Kidderminster Harriers, signing professional forms in March 1926. A month later, he won a junior international cap against Scotland but had to wait until the following season before making his first-team debut. A regular for four seasons, he lost his place for the 1930–31 and 1931–32 campaigns, but returned the following season to play until 1936. He joined Southampton, having played in 241 league and Cup games for Villa, but after a little over a season injury forced his retirement and he went into management, first with Yeovil Town and then Weymouth.

KIRTON, BILLY. Billy Kirton cost Aston Villa £500 when he was one of a number of Leeds City players auctioned off after the club had become defunct. He made his Villa debut in the 4–1 win at Middlesbrough in October 1919 and at the end of that season scored the winning goal in the FA Cup final against Huddersfield Town which Villa won 1–0. In October 1921, Kirton made his one and only appearance for England, scoring their goal in a 1–1 draw with Ireland in Belfast. In 1924, he won an FA Cup runners-up medal when Villa lost 2–0 to Newcastle United and played the last of his 261 first-team games against West Ham United in April 1927. He joined Coventry City in September of the following year. After making just 16 appearances for Coventry, he ended his playing days in non-league football, first with Kidderminster Harriers and then Leamington Town.

L

LARGEST CROWD. It was on 2 March 1946 that Villa Park housed its largest crowd. The occasion was the FA Cup sixth-round match against Derby County. A staggering crowd of 76,588 saw Villa go down 4–3 to the Rams, with Edwards, Iverson and Broome scoring the home side's goals.

LATE FINISHES. Villa's final match of the season against Stoke City at Villa Park on 26 May 1947 is the latest date for the finish of any Aston Villa season. When Villa won the European Cup in 1982, that match against Bayern Munich was also played on 26 May.

LEADING GOALSCORERS. Aston Villa have provided the Football League's divisional leading goalscorer on eight occasions. They are:

1895–96	Johnny Campbell	division one	20
1897–98	Fred Wheldon	division one	21
1899–00	Billy Garraty	division one	27
1911–12	Harry Hampton	division one	25
1930–31	Tom Waring	division one	49
1974–75	Brian Little	division two	20
1976–77	Andy Gray	division one	25

1980–81	Peter Withe	division one	20

LEAGUE CUP. See Football League Cup.

LEAGUE GOALS – CAREER HIGHEST. Harry Hampton holds the Villa record for the most league goals with a career total of 215 goals scored between 1904 and 1920.

LEAGUE GOALS – LEAST CONCEDED. When Villa won the third division championship in 1971–2, they conceded just 32 goals in 46 games. They also conceded 32 in 1974–75 when they won promotion to the first division as runners-up to Manchester United.

LEAGUE GOALS – MOST INDIVIDUAL. Tom 'Pongo' Waring holds the Villa record for the most league goals in a season with 49 scored in the first division during the 1930–31 season.

LEAGUE GOALS – MOST SCORED. Villa's highest goal tally in the Football League was achieved during the 1930–31 season when they finished as runners-up to Arsenal in the first division and scored 128 goals.

LEAGUE VICTORY – HIGHEST. Villa's best Football League victory was the 12–2 win over Accrington at Villa Park on 12 March 1892. John Devey and Johnny Campbell both scored four goals. The other scorers were Billy Dickson 2, Dennis Hodgetts and Charlie Athersmith. On 24 November 1959, Villa beat Charlton Athletic 11–1 with Gerry Hitchens scoring five goals. Villa also had two other League victories when they scored double figures. Both were 10–0 victories, one over Sheffield Wednesday on 5 October 1912, the other over Burnley on the opening day of the 1925–26 season.

LEAKE, ALEX. One of the most popular Villa players in the early part of the 20th century, Alex Leake began his professional career with Small Heath, appearing in 199 league games for the club. He moved to Villa in the summer of 1902 and made his league debut at Nottingham Forest in September of the following season. He was an important member of Villa's FA Cup winning side of 1905 and won the first of five full caps for England in 1904 in a 1–0 win at Celtic Park. He played in 141 league and Cup games for Villa, his last being a 2–2 draw against Manchester City in November 1907. He had three years with Burnley before signing for Wednesbury Old Athletic. In 1912, he joined Crystal Palace as trainer and despite being 40 years of age, was selected as England's reserve. When he left Villa Park, Leake was presented with a shield in appreciation of his magnificent service to the club.

LEE, GORDON. Left-back Gordon Lee signed professional forms for Aston Villa in October 1955 but completed his National Service in the RAF before returning to play for the club two years later. He made his debut at home to Nottingham Forest in September 1958, going on to appear in 142 first-team games for the club. He won a League Cup winners' tankard in 1961 and a runners-up medal in the same competition two years later, but in 1966 he left Villa Park to become player-coach at Shrewsbury Town. In 1968, he was appointed manager of Port Vale and took them up to the third division before joining Blackburn Rovers and winning promotion to the second division for the Ewood Park club in their centenary year. He led Newcastle United to the League Cup and into Europe before taking over at Everton in January 1977. He built a side of considerable ability, but they were beaten by Villa in the League Cup final in his first season at Goodison and after four years in charge he lost his job. After managing Preston North End and Reykjavik of Iceland, he worked with David Pleat at Leicester City, eventually becoming caretaker manager before being sacked, despite steering the Filberts clear of relegation.

LEONARD, KEITH. After an unsuccessful trial with West Bromwich Albion, Keith Leonard turned his attention to the non-league game and played for Kidderminster Harriers, Darlaston and Highgate United before signing professional forms for Aston Villa in April 1972. After a spell of sustained scoring in the reserves, he made a couple of first-team appearances as substitute before suffering a double fracture of his right leg in a car crash. Twelve months later in December 1973, he went on loan to Port Vale, where he scored just one goal in 12 league appearances for the Valiants. He returned to Villa Park to become an important member of the team that won the League Cup and promotion from the second division. He started the 1975–76 season well with three goals in seven appearances when he damaged his troublesome right knee in the match against Arsenal in September and never recovered from the injury. Aged only 24, Villa made him coach and after a testimonial in 1978, he coached at Birmingham City and West Bromwich Albion, both under the managership of former Villa boss, Ron Saunders.

LITTLE, BRIAN. Born in Durham City, Brian Little joined Aston Villa as an apprentice in 1969, turning professional two years later. He made his first-team debut as a substitute at home to Blackburn Rovers on 30 October 1971. On his first full first-team appearance in April of the following year, he scored one of the goals in a 5–1 win over Torquay United. Little was still only 17 and played an important part in the club's FA Youth Cup success when they beat Liverpool in the final. Little went on to win League Cup winners' tankards in

Brian Little

1975 and 1977, scoring two of Villa's goals in the 3-2 win over Everton in the third match of that final at Old Trafford. In fact, his match-winner came in the dying seconds of injury time. He was the second division's leading goalscorer in 1974–75 with 20 goals, including a hat-trick in the 5-0 win over Oldham Athletic. At the end of that season, he won his only full cap for England in what was one of the briefest debuts ever at international level. Replacing Mick Channon against Wales at Wembley with just ten minutes to play, he helped set up England's second goal for David Johnson. During the 1979-80 season, a proposed £610,000 move to neighbours and rivals Birmingham City fell through on medical grounds and sadly, at the end of the following season, he was forced to give up the game. He had scored 82 goals in 301 first-team appearances. He had a spell working in the club's promotion department but moved to Molineux as first-team coach before replacing Sammy Chapman. He lost out to Graham Turner a few weeks later and joined former Villa team-mate Bruce Rioch at Middlesbrough before leaving to manage Darlington. He led the Quakers to the GM Vauxhall Conference title and back into the Football League, where they won the fourth division championship. He then took charge at Leicester City and after three successive seasons of reaching the Wembley play-off finals, the Filberts eventually won promotion to the Premiership. In November 1994, Little returned to Villa as manager and after struggling throughout the season, the club secured Premiership safety on the final day of the campaign. The following season, he set about rebuilding the Villa side and was rewarded with victory in the League Cup final at Wembley.

LITTLEWOODS CUP. See Football League Cup.

LOCHHEAD, ANDY. A striker with a deadly finish, Scottish-born Andy Lochhead began his league career with Burnley, making his debut in 1958. He had a fine career at Turf Moor, for in the ten years he spent with the East Lancashire club, he scored 101 goals in 226 league appearances before joining Leicester City. He appeared in the 1969 FA Cup final for the Filbert Street club, moving to Aston Villa in February 1970. He played in the League Cup final against Tottenham Hotspur the following year and in 1971–72 won a third division championship medal. That season, he headed the club's goalscoring charts with 19, including a hat-trick in a 6–0 win at Oldham Athletic, the club he joined after leaving Villa Park in the summer of 1973. After Oldham, he played in the NASL before returning to Boundary Park as coach and then Turf Moor as scout.

LONG SERVICE. A number of the club's illustrious personalities have given long service to the club. George Ramsay captained Villa to their first trophy success in 1880, when they won the Birmingham Senior Cup. After playing his first game in 1876, he was forced to leave the game six years later through injury. From 1884 until 1926 he served the club as secretary. John Devey played for Villa from 1891 to 1902, scoring 187 goals in 306 appearances before retiring. He was immediately elected to the Villa board and continued to serve the club in that capacity until 1934. Howard Spencer signed for Villa in 1894 and was a regular member of the side until 1907. Two years later, he was voted on to the Villa board and remained in office until the summer of 1936. Eric Houghton is one of the greatest names in the club's history. He scored 170 goals for Villa in 392 first-team games between 1930 and 1946, before returning to the club in 1953 as manager. He lost that position a year and a half after seeing Villa beat Manchester United in the FA Cup final of 1957.

LOST. When Aston Villa won the FA Cup in 1895, they were approached by a Mr W. Shillcock, a football and football boot manufacturer, with a request to allow him to display the trophy in his shop window at 73, Newton Row, Birmingham. Permission was granted but on that fateful night, 11 September 1895, the trophy disappeared without trace. The truth about the Cup's eventual whereabouts has never really been established, although in 1958 an 83-year-old man owned up to the theft. He maintained he had melted it down to make counterfeit coins, but his story was never substantiated. However, Villa were fined £25 and a new trophy had to be acquired.

LOWE, EDDIE. Born in Halesowen, Eddie Lowe guested for Millwall, Finchley and Walthamstow Avenue during the Second World War but after returning to the Midlands to play in the Birmingham and District League, he was signed by Villa in the summer of 1945. A skilful wing-half, he was the first post-war Villa player to win an international cap when he played for England against France at Highbury in May 1947. He played in a further two internationals that year but at Villa Park he found himself in and out of the side and in May 1950 he left Villa for Fulham. At Craven Cottage over the next 13 seasons, he appeared in well over 500 league and Cup games, helping them gain promotion to the first division in 1958–59. He later spent a couple of seasons as player-manager of Notts County before leaving the game.

LOWEST. The lowest number of goals scored by Aston Villa in a single Football League season is 36 in 1969–70. The club's lowest points record in the Football League occurred in 1890–91 when Villa gained just 18 points from 22 matches. The club's lowest points tally from a 42-match programme is 29 in seasons 1966–67 and 1969–70, the club being relegated on both occasions.

LYNN, STAN. Born in Bolton, right-back Stan Lynn began his league career with Accrington Stanley, from whom Villa signed him for £10,000 in March 1951. Though he made his first-team debut almost immediately, it was the 1954–55 season before he established himself in the Villa team. Possessing a powerful shot, Lynn scored 38 goals for the Villans, the majority from free kicks or penalties, and on 11 January 1958, he scored a hat-trick in a 5–2 win over Sunderland, the first full-back to achieve such a feat in a first division game. With Villa he appeared in 323 games, helping the club win the FA Cup in 1957, the second division championship in 1960 and the League Cup in 1961, although he played in only the first leg of the two-legged final. In October 1961, he moved across the city to St Andrews where he played in 131 league games, scoring 26 goals. In 1963 he was in the Blues side that beat Villa in the final of the League Cup.

LYONS, TOM. Signing professional forms for Villa in 1907, Tom Lyons made his debut in a 5–0 defeat at Anfield. Things could only get better and the following week he was outstanding in Villa's 6–0 demolition of Middlesbrough. A hard-tackling full-back, quick to cover his partner, he went on to play in 237 first-team games for Villa, his last being in a 2–2 draw at Bradford in April 1915. He never played football after the First World War.

M

MacEWAN, JIMMY. Scotsman Jimmy MacEwan began his career with Arbroath just after the Second World War, moving on to Raith Rovers in 1950. At Starks Park, he was the club's leading goalscorer for three successive seasons from 1956 to 1959. During his last season with the club, 1958–59, he represented the Scottish League and was selected as a reserve for the full national side. He joined Villa in July 1959 and made his debut in the opening game of the following season, scoring the first goal in the club's 2–1 win at Brighton and Hove Albion. That season Villa won the second division championship and MacEwan's wing play was a major factor in the club achieving that goal. In 1960–61, MacEwan played a big part in the club reaching the League Cup final. They reached it again two years later but by this time MacEwan had lost his place in the side. He left the club to play for Walsall where, after just ten league appearances, he was appointed the club's trainer.

MacLEOD, JOHNNY. Edinburgh-born winger Johnny MacLeod started his career with Hibernian, leaving the Easter Road club for Arsenal in June 1961. He represented the Scottish League and won four full caps for Scotland just prior to his move to Highbury. For the Gunners, he scored 23 goals in 110 league appearances before signing for Aston Villa for £29,500 in

September 1964. An instant hit with the Villa fans, the diminutive winger possessed speed and skill and was a first-team regular for four years until losing his place to Willie Anderson. He left Villa to play in Belgium with KV Mechelen before ending his career back in Scotland with Raith Rovers.

MANAGERS. This is a complete list of Villa's full-time managers with the inclusive dates during which they held office.

1934–36	Jimmy McMullan	1970–74	Vic Crowe
1936–39	Jimmy Hogan	1974–82	Ron Saunders
1945–50	Alex Massie	1982–84	Tony Barton
1950–53	George Martin	1984–86	Graham Turner
1953–58	Eric Houghton	1986–87	Billy McNeill
1958–64	Joe Mercer	1987–90	Graham Taylor
1964–67	Dick Taylor	1990–91	Jozef Venglos
1967–68	Tommy Cummings	1991–94	Ron Atkinson
1968–70	Tommy Docherty	1994–	Brian Little

MANDLEY, JACK. A tricky winger with a powerful shot, Jack Mandley played his early football in the North Staffordshire Sunday Schools League, from where Port Vale secured his services as an amateur. He had scored six goals in 47 appearances for the Vale Park club when Villa persuaded him to join them midway through the 1929–30 season. He repaid a slice of the £7,000 transfer fee by scoring Villa's opening goal on his debut in a 5–3 win over Huddersfield Town. He played in 112 league and Cup games for Villa, scoring 26 goals. He retired in 1934 following the arrival of Cunliffe and Dix at Villa Park.

MARATHON MATCHES. During the 1954–55 season, Aston Villa were involved in five matches against Doncaster Rovers in the fourth round of the FA Cup. The first match at Belle Vue was goalless, whilst two goals from Tommy Thompson gave Villa a 2–2 draw after extra-time in the replay. In the third meeting at Manchester City's Maine Road, Thompson scored again for Villa in a 1–1 draw. The fourth match at Hillsborough resulted in another goalless ninety minutes but in the fifth match, three weeks after the original game, Villa went down 3–1 at the Hawthorns with Johnny Dixon netting their goal.

MARKSMEN – LEAGUE. Villa's top league goalscorer is Harry Hampton who struck 215 goals during his 12 seasons at Villa Park. Only seven players have hit more than 100 league goals for the club.

1.	Harry Hampton	215	6.	Tom Waring	159
2.	Billy Walker	214	7.	Johnny Dixon	132
3.	John Devey	169	8.	Peter McParland	97
4.	Joe Bache	168	9.	Billy Garraty	96
5.	Eric Houghton	160	10.	Dai Astley	92

MARKSMEN – OVERALL. Ten players have hit a hundred goals for Aston Villa. The club's top marksman is Billy Walker. The Century Club consists of:

1.	Billy Walker	244	6.	Johnny Dixon	144
2.	Harry Hampton	242	7.	Peter McParland	120
3.	John Devey	187	8.	Billy Garraty	112
4.	Joe Bache	185	9.	Dai Astley	100
5.	Eric Houghton	170	10.	Len Capewell	100

MARTIN, CON. After playing his early football in Ireland with Drumcondra and Glentoran, Con Martin made his Football League debut for Leeds United, whom he joined in December 1946. Converted into a centre-half, he won international honours for both Northern Ireland and the Republic of Ireland, appearing in six and 30 games respectively for the two countries. He transferred to Aston Villa in September 1948 and made his debut in a 4–3 win over Sheffield United. He scored only one goal in his 213 games for the club, and that was from the penalty spot in a 4–1 win at Charlton Athletic, but the versatile Martin played 27 of his games in goal. He left the club in the summer of 1956 to become player-manager of Waterford.

MARTIN, GEORGE. A fast, powerful and versatile player, George Martin scored 56 goals in 204 appearances for Hull City before moving to Everton, where he helped the Goodison Park club to win the second division championship in 1930–31. During the Second World War, he took over as manager of Luton Town but it was with Newcastle United, whom he led to the second division title in 1947–48, that he first made his name. Despite taking the Magpies into the top six of the first division, he could not settle at St James' Park and in December 1950, he moved to Villa Park. He had an awkward relationship with the Villa board and in August 1953, left in controversial circumstances when he was forced to resign. He later returned to management with Luton Town after a spell as their chief scout, but it was an unhappy experience as the Hatters were relegated to the fourth division.

MASSIE, ALEX. Born in Glasgow, Alex Massie played for Partick Thistle and Ayr United before Bury paid £1,000 to bring the talented wing-half into the Football League. Not retained by the Gigg Lane club, he went to work in America before going to live in Ireland where he played for the Dublin Dolphins. His career only really took off when he returned to Scotland having signed for Hearts. In 1931, he won the first of his 18 Scottish caps. He skippered his country in 1935, and played his last game for the Tynecastle club. He signed for Aston Villa in December 1935 for a fee of £6,000 and in his first three games Villa conceded 17 goals. Villa were relegated at the end of that season but in 1937–38 returned to the top flight as champions of the second division with Massie playing an important role in the club's revival. During the war, Massie played in 131 games for Villa, winning a Football League Cup (North) medal in 1944. Not a prolific scorer by any stretch of the imagination, he hit five goals in a 14–1 wartime win over RAF (Hednesford). In September 1945, Massie retired from playing to become Villa manager. He stayed in the job for five years before joining Torquay United in a similar capacity.

McGRATH, PAUL. Born of Irish parents in Ealing, London, Paul McGrath was discovered by Manchester United playing for St Patrick's Athletic in the League of Ireland. He made his debut for the Reds against Tottenham Hotspur on 13 November 1982 and eventually gained a regular first-team place. He won an FA Cup winners' medal in 1985 when United beat Everton at Wembley. Earlier that season he won the first of his many full caps for the Republic of Ireland when he came on as a substitute against Italy. Despite being injured for much of the 1987–88 season, he recovered in time to star in the Irish midfield during the 1988

European Championships. Injuries again took their toll the following season and in August 1989, he joined Aston Villa for £400,000. He proved to be an exceptional signing for Villa, helping them to the runners-up spot in the first division in 1989–90. McGrath represented the Football League and was the mainstay of Jack Charlton's Republic of Ireland side that qualified for the 1990 World Cup finals. He had a superb season for Villa in 1991–92, missing just one game and was voted the PFA Player of the Year. He was just as outstanding the following season as Villa finished runners-up to his old club

Paul McGrath

Manchester United in the battle for the first Premier league championship. He continued to play on borrowed time – his past injuries being sure to catch up with him – and had played in 322 first-team games for the Villans when he was allowed to join Premiership rivals, Derby County.

McMAHON, PAT. A childhood supporter of Celtic, he joined the Parkhead club from Kilsyth Rangers in 1967 and though he only appeared in three league games in two seasons with them he was bitterly disappointed when they released him in the summer of 1969. Villa signed him on a free transfer, just beating Dunfermline for his services, and over the next six seasons, he played in 149 league and Cup games, scoring 30 goals. He was a member of Villa's League Cup final side that lost to Tottenham Hotspur in 1971 and of the side that won the third division championship the following season. He left Villa Park in 1976, joining NASL club Portland Timbers with goalkeeper Jim Cumbes.

McMULLAN, JIMMY. As a player with Third Lanark, Partick Thistle and Manchester City, Jimmy McMullan won 16 full caps for Scotland, played four times for the Scottish League and appeared in four Victory Internationals in 1919. With Partick Thistle, he won a Scottish Cup winners' medal and, with Manchester, he collected FA Cup runners-up medals in 1926 and 1933 and a second division championship medal in 1927–28. He captained Scotland when the Wembley Wizards beat England at Wembley in 1928. Appointed manager of Oldham Athletic in 1933, he spent only a year at Boundary Park before joining Aston Villa as the club's first-team manager. Unfortunately, at the end of the 1935–36 season, the club were relegated for the first time in their history and in October 1936 he was sacked. He went on to manage Notts County before ending his involvement with the game as secretary-manager of Sheffield Wednesday.

McNAUGHT, KEN. A tough, rugged Scot, Ken McNaught joined Everton straight from school, making his league debut towards the end of the 1974–75 season. In 1976–77, he was Everton's only ever-present, playing in all 58 competitive matches and playing against Villa in the League Cup final of that season. After 86 appearances for the Goodison Park club, he joined Aston Villa for £200,000 and soon established himself alongside Leighton Phillips in the heart of the Villa defence. After that first season, he was partnered by Allan Evans and in 1980–81 when Villa won the league championship, McNaught was ever present. The following campaign saw him win a European Cup winners' medal and in 1982, a European Super Cup winners' medal. He played in 259 first-team games for Villa before being allowed to join former Villa player, Ron Wylie, at West Bromwich

Ken McNaught

113

Albion for £125,000. After appearing in every league and Cup game for the Hawthorns club in 1983–84, he lost his place and went on loan to Manchester City before signing for Sheffield United. A year later, he was forced to retire through injury and in 1987 he was appointed coach to Dunfermline Athletic.

McNEILL, BILLY. A commanding centre-half, Billy McNeill was a born leader. His decision to retire in 1975 brought to an end one of the most successful club careers of any British footballer. He made a traumatic debut for Scotland in the 9–3 defeat by England at Wembley in 1961, but played in 831 games for Celtic, which included their 1967 European Cup final triumph. McNeill collected 23 major winners' medals and in 1974 was awarded the MBE for services to football. He moved into management with Clyde in April 1977 but within a couple of months had joined Aberdeen. In May 1978 he moved back to Parkhead where he took over from Jock Stein. He stayed there for five years, winning more trophies before moving to Manchester City. He took the Maine Road club to promotion to division one in 1985 and to a Full Members Cup final appearance at Wembley where they lost 5–4 to Chelsea. In September 1986 he took charge at Aston Villa but at the end of the season they were relegated along with Manchester City and McNeill was sacked. After his dismissal he moved back to Parkhead to manage Celtic before handing the job over to Liam Brady.

McPARLAND, PETER. One of the club's greatest goalscoring wingers, Peter McParland joined Aston Villa from League of Ireland club, Dundalk for £3,880 in the summer of 1952. He was capped by Northern Ireland on 34 occasions, scoring both goals on his debut against Wales in 1954 when the Irish won 2–1 at Wrexham. McParland was also the scorer of both Villa goals when they beat Manchester United 2–1 to win the 1957 FA Cup. In 1958, he represented Northern Ireland in the World Cup finals in Sweden and in 1960 he won a second division championship medal with Villa and represented the Football League against the Italian League. In the two-legged League Cup final of 1961, he scored the winner against Rotherham United. He topped the club's goalscoring charts in 1956–57 but his best season in terms of goals scored was 1959–60 when he scored 25 league and Cup goals in 46 appearances. He left Wolverhampton Wanderers in January 1962 after scoring 120 goals in 340 games. A year later he joined Plymouth Argyle, then Worcester City, before managing Glentoran. He had a spell at Bournemouth but has since spent most of his time coaching abroad.

MERCER, JOE. Joe Mercer had a great career, both as a player and a manager. An outstanding wing-half, he gained three league championship medals, played in two FA Cup finals for Arsenal and appeared five times for his country. He started his career with Everton and won his first league championship medal with them in 1938–39. He played regularly in wartime soccer, being part of a famous England half-back line with Stan Cullis and Cliff Britton. Finding himself out of favour at Goodison Park, he joined Arsenal for £7,000 in November 1946. He had made 184 league and Cup appearances for Everton and over the next eight seasons made another 293 with the Gunners. As well as his league championship and FA Cup successes with the Highbury club, he was voted Footballer of the Year in 1950. In April 1954, he broke his leg and this brought his playing career to an end. His first managerial post was at Sheffield United, but in December 1958, he left to become manager at Aston Villa. He failed to save the club from relegation that season, but soon changed their fortunes around as they took the second division championship in 1959–60. He led Villa to League Cup finals in 1961 and 1963 but in 1964, he suffered a stroke due to overwork and had to retire. However, a year later, he joined Manchester City and with his assistant Malcolm Allison brought the good times back to Maine Road. The club won the second division title in 1965–66, the league championship two years later, the FA Cup in 1969 and the European Cup-Winners' Cup in 1970. In 1972 he became general manager at Coventry City and in 1974 caretaker manager of England after Don Revie's resignation. He lived in the Merseyside area until his death in 1990.

MILES, FREDDIE. Signed from Aston St Marys where he played his early football, full-back Freddie Miles made his Villa debut in the 7–3 win at Nottingham Forest on 19 December 1903. During his first season at Villa Park, he developed a fine understanding with Howard Spencer and in 1905 won an FA Cup winners' medal as Villa beat Newcastle United 2–0 at the Crystal Palace. When Spencer lost his place to Tommy Lyons, the two emerged as probably the best full-back pairing in the first division and went a long way in helping Villa win the league championship in 1909–10. Very popular with the Villa fans, Miles played in 269 league and Cup games before retiring in the summer of 1914 to become the club's trainer.

MILNE, VIC. A medical student at Aberdeen University, Vic Milne's studies were interrupted by the First World War as he was called up to serve in the Royal Engineers. After the hostilities had ended, he continued with his studies, graduating as a doctor in 1921. During this time, the Scottish-born defender played for Aberdeen, holding his place in the Dons' line-up for three seasons. Joining Villa in 1923, he played in the FA Cup final at the end of his first season but unfortunately Villa lost 2–0 to Newcastle United. The club's regular centre-half for six seasons, Milne played in 175 first-team games before deciding to retire at the age of 32 to concentrate on his profession. He later became the club's official doctor.

MILOSEVIC, SAVO. Signed by Brian Little in the summer of 1995, Savo Milosevic joined the club for £3.5 million simply on the strength of a video. The little-known Serbian forward from Partizan Belgrade displayed tremendous ability but failed to score in his first ten games at Villa Park. When he did open his account, he hit a hat-trick in the 4–1 defeat of Coventry City on 16 December 1995. He scored 14 times that season, despite some occasional erratic finishing. One of his goals was a brilliant solo effort to open Villa's account in the League Cup final against Leeds United. There were rumours that the popular Serb wanted to leave Villa Park but these were scotched and Milosevic is still displaying his impressive skills for Villa.

MORLEY, TONY. Born in Ormskirk, winger Tony Morley began his league career with Preston North End, making 99 appearances for the Lilywhites before being transferred to Burnley for £100,000. At Turf Moor, Morley played in 100 first-team games and despite impressing a number of top clubs, it was Aston Villa who signed him in June 1979 for £200,000. In 1980–81, he was an ever-present as Villa won the first division championship, scoring 10 goals as well as making many more for Withe and Shaw. The following season, he won the first of six international caps and Villa won the European Cup and in 1982–83, the European Super Cup. In December 1983, after playing in 179 first-team games and scoring 34 goals, he joined neighbours West Bromwich Albion for £75,000. Unable to settle at the Hawthorns, he had loan spells with Birmingham City and Hong Kong side FC Seiko before being sold to FC Den Haag of Holland. After helping

Tony Morley

the Dutch side win promotion to their first division, former Villa boss Ron Saunders brought him back to the Hawthorns for a second spell.

MORT, TOMMY. Born at Kearsley, near Bolton, Tommy Mort started his career as a semi-professional with non-league Altrincham before joining Rochdale as a professional in the summer of 1921. Villa signed him the following April and he made his debut in the 2–1 defeat of his home town club, Bolton Wanderers, a couple of days later. Forming a solid full-back pairing with Tommy Smart, Mort went on to serve Villa until 1935, playing in 368 first-team games. He was capped three times by England, winning his first against Wales in 1924, the year he appeared for Villa in the FA Cup final against Newcastle United. Renowned for his sliding tackle, he scored just two goals in his time at Villa, the second coming in the 7–1 win over Middlesbrough on Christmas Day 1931.

MORTIMER, DENNIS. Captain of Villa when they won the league championship in 1980–81, Dennis Mortimer joined

117

Coventry City's apprentice staff in the summer of 1967. The talented midfielder played in 220 first-team games for the Highfield Road club before joining Villa for £175,000 in December 1975. With the Villans, Mortimer won a League Cup winners' tankard in 1977 and winners' medals in the club's successes in the first division, European Cup and European Super Cup competitions in 1981 and 1982. He won Youth and Under-23 caps for England before captaining England 'B' in Australia in 1980 and was desperately unlucky not to win full international honours. An ever-present for Villa in seasons 1977–78 and 1980-81, he appeared in 404 matches, scoring 36 goals before joining Brighton and Hove Albion at the end of the 1984–85 season. He had a season with Birmingham City in 1986–87 but then retired from league football.

MORTON, HARRY. After unsuccessful trials with Bury and Bolton Wanderers, goalkeeper Harry Morton went into the Army. In 1930, he played for the Army against Villa in a friendly and, even though Villa won 7–0, impressed enough to be offered a trial with the Colts. He signed professional forms in March 1931 but had to wait for his league debut which came in unusual circumstances. Villa's regular keeper Fred Biddlestone was injured during the pre-match kick-in against Manchester City in November 1933 and Morton was summoned from the Maine Road stand to replace him. After helping his side earn a point in a 3–3 draw, he missed just one of the next 163 matches, appearing in 98 consecutive games for the club. In March 1937 he joined Everton, playing in 29 games for the Toffees before ending his league career with Burnley.

MOSS, FRANK senior. Joining Villa in February 1914, Frank Moss appeared in just two league games before the First World War interrupted his career. During the war, he served with the 4th Lincolnshire Regiment but was severely wounded in his left knee

Frank Moss snr

and sent home. He became a PE instructor. His wound healed and when football resumed in 1919, he was back at Villa Park. At the end of his first full season, he replaced the injured Jimmy Harrop in the FA Cup win over Huddersfield Town, blotting out the Terriers' twin strike-force of Mann and Taylor. He won five full caps for England, his first against Scotland at Villa Park in April 1922. He continued to play for Villa until 1929 when, after appearing in 283 first-team games, he joined Cardiff City before becoming player-manager of Bromsgrove Rovers a few months later.

MOSS, FRANK junior. Frank Moss junior was a resolute centre-half who made his Villa debut at home to Everton in 1938–39, the last full season of league football before the war. During the hostilities, he guested for Birmingham City and Northampton Town before returning to Villa Park where he became the club's first choice in that pivotal role for the next eight seasons. An ever-present in 1949–50, one of the three league goals he scored in his career was enough to take both points in the match against Manchester City. He went on to play in 314 first-team games for Villa before his retirement from the game in 1955. His career was ended early by a Duncan Edwards tackle in Villa's 1–0 win at Old Trafford on 27 December 1954. In fact, he made one more appearance in the Villa side at Charlton Athletic, but after the club's 6–1 defeat he hung up his boots.

MOST MATCHES. Aston Villa played their most matches, 60, in the 1981–82 season. This comprised 42 league games, three FA Cup games, six Football League Cup games and nine European Cup games when they won the trophy.

MOUNTFIELD, DEREK. After playing in only 30 games for fourth division Tranmere Rovers, Derek Mountfield joined Everton, the club he had supported as a schoolboy, for £30,000 in June 1982. Within five years at Goodison Park, he had gained an FA Cup winners' medal, two league championship medals, a European Cup-Winners' Cup medal and two Charity Shield medals, not to mention caps for England at 'B' and Under-21 level. During Everton's magnificent 1984–85 season, he scored 14 goals from the centre-half position, including the last-minute equaliser against Ipswich Town in the FA Cup quarter-final and the semi-final extra-time winner against Luton Town at Villa Park. Following the arrival of Dave Watson, he moved to Villa in June 1988 for £450,000. Though injuries hampered his first season with the club, he established himself alongside Kent Nielsen, but following the signing of Shaun Teale from Bournemouth, he lost his place and after playing in 120 games and scoring 17 goals, he moved to Molineux to play for Wolverhampton Wanderers. In 1994 he joined Carlisle United and was a key member of their 1994–95 championship-winning season. He later played for Northampton Town before signing for Walsall.

MULRANEY, AMBROSE. A clever two-footed winger, Jock Mulraney signed professional forms for Celtic, but despite playing for the Scottish Alliance XI, he never really settled at Parkhead and after trials with a number of clubs, he joined Dartford before signing for Ipswich Town in 1936. The following season, he helped the club win the southern league championship and in April 1939 he scored the Portman Road club's first-ever Football League hat-trick against Bristol City. There is no doubt that he would have won international honours had it not been for the war but in 1945 he joined Birmingham City and helped them win the league championship (south) the following year. He had short spells with Shrewsbury Town and Kidderminster Harriers before joining Aston Villa in September 1948. He had appeared in only 12 league matches for the Villans when he suffered an Achilles tendon injury which ended his career.

MURDER. On 10 November 1923, Tommy Ball, Aston Villa's young centre-half was shot dead outside his home in Perry Barr. So far as anyone knows, that gives Tommy Ball the unfortunate distinction of being the only professional footballer to have been murdered. He had played in 14 of the first 16 matches that season and had been outstanding at the heart of the Villa defence in the previous day's match against Notts County, which Villa won 1–0. George Stagg, Ball's landlord and neighbour and a former member of the Birmingham Police Force, was arrested and charged with the murder. Found guilty, he was sentenced to death in February 1924 and executed at Stafford. Ball's funeral took place at St John's Church, Perry Barr, on 19 November 1923. Thousands of Villa fans lined the route while the coffin was carried to the church and then the grave by Villa's first-team players. A lasting tribute to this fine player takes the form of a granite football in St John's churchyard.

N

NEAL, JOHN. Signed for Hull City by Raich Carter, John Neal played in 60 league games for the Tigers before signing for Swindon Town in July 1957. Two years later, he left the County Ground for Aston Villa and after missing the opening match of the 1959–60 season played in all the rest, winning a second division championship medal. He also won a League Cup winners' tankard in 1961, but a year later he left Villa Park after playing in 114 league and Cup games to join Southend United. After his playing days were over, he managed Wrexham, leading them to promotion from the fourth division in 1970 and to victory in the Welsh Cup final in 1972 and 1975. Perhaps his best performance as Wrexham manager was to lead the club into the quarter-finals of the European Cup-Winners' Cup in 1976. He later managed Middlesbrough and Chelsea, taking the Stamford Bridge side to the second division championship in 1984.

NEUTRAL GROUNDS. Whilst Villa Park has been used as a neutral ground for FA Cup replays, FA Cup semi-finals and a Football League Cup final replay, Aston Villa themselves have had to replay on a neutral ground a number of times. One of the most important occasions was the 3–2 League Cup final second replay win over Everton at Old Trafford in April 1977. Having drawn 0–0 at Wembley, an own goal from Everton's Roger Kenyon gave them a draw at Hillsborough before goals from Chris Nicholl and Brian Little (2) gave them victory at the third attempt. All the club's FA Cup semi-finals were of course played on neutral grounds. Of their 20 appearances including replays in this stage of the competition, six were held at Bramall Lane, two each at the City Ground and Ewood Park and one each at the Baseball Ground, Goodison Park, Victoria Ground, White Hart Lane, Highbury, Leeds Road, Molineux, St Andrews, Hillsborough and the Hawthorns. FA Cup final appearances have been at The Oval, Crystal Palace, Stamford Bridge and Wembley, and the European Cup final win over Bayern Munich took place in Rotterdam.

NIBLOE, JOE. Full-back Joe Nibloe spent eight years with Kilmarnock, where he won a Scottish Cup winners' medal in 1929, before moving to Aston Villa in September 1932. A Scottish international, he won 11 caps before joining Villa and represented the Scottish League. He made his Villa debut in a 4–2 win over Wolverhampton Wanderers at Molineux and played in 12 games as the club ended the season as runners-up in the first division. A regular during the 1933–34 season, he surprisingly joined Sheffield Wednesday in part-exchange for George Beeson in the close season and the following year had a good game as the Owls beat West Bromwich Albion in the FA Cup final. He made 128 first-team appearances for Wednesday before hanging up his boots to become the club's junior coach.

NICHOLL, CHRIS. Chris Nicholl played his first Football League games for Halifax Town after joining the Shaymen from non-league Witton Albion in the summer of 1968. His next move was to Luton Town where he was an important member of the Hatters' defence when they won promotion from the third division. He joined Aston Villa in March 1972 for £75,000 replacing former Coventry centre-half, George Curtis. He played in the last 13 games of that season, grabbing an all-important equalising goal in his second game at Shrewsbury to help Villa win the third division championship. He won two League Cup winners' tankards with Villa, scoring one of the goals that defeated Everton in the third meeting between the two clubs in the 1977 final. Chris Nicholl won 51 caps for Northern Ireland, his first coming against Sweden in 1975. In 1976, the popular centre-half managed to score all four goals in a 2–2 draw against Leicester City at Filbert Street. After playing in 250 games for Villa, Nicholl joined Southampton in the summer of 1977 and helped them return to the top flight at the end of his first season. He also appeared for the Saints in the League Cup final of 1979 and in Europe during the early '80s. He played in 228 league games for Southampton before signing for Grimsby Town, where he stayed for two years. He returned to the Dell as manager in July 1985, replacing Lawrie McMenemy, but lost his job at the end of the 1990–91 season. He is now manager of Walsall.

NICKNAMES. Aston Villa's nickname is the Villans. Many players in the club's history have been fondly known by their nicknames, including:

1880–86	Arthur Brown–Digger
1893–97	Jack Reynolds–Baldy
1896–1900	Fred Wheldon–Diamond
1904–20	Harry Hampton–Wellington Whirlwind
1914–29	Frank Moss senior–Snowy
1927–36	Tom Waring–Pongo
1929–34	George Brown–Bomber
1933–47	Ernie Callaghan–Mush
1935–49	George Cummings–Icicle
1946–54	Billy Goffin–Cowboy
1961–67	John Sleeuwenhoek–Tulip
1969–76	Ian Hamilton–Chico

The full-back pairing of Tommy Smart (1919–32) and Tommy Mort (1921–35) were known as Death and Glory.

NON-LEAGUE. In their early years, Villa met non-league opposition in the FA Cup on a number of occasions, resulting in some fairly heavy defeats for the amateur sides: 13–1 v the Casuals on 17 January 1891 and 11–0 v Kings Lynn on 13 January 1906. The most recent game against non-league opposition in the FA Cup came on 25 January 1996 when Gravesend were beaten 3–0 in a third-round tie with goals from Draper, Milosevic and Johnson.

O

OLDEST PLAYER. The oldest player to line-up in an Aston Villa team is Ernie Callaghan. He was 39 years 257 days old when he played his last game for the club against Grimsby Town (home 3–3) on 12 April 1947.

OLNEY, BEN. Beginning his league career with Derby County, goalkeeper Ben Olney was a constant fixture in the team following his debut in May 1921. However, after helping the club win promotion to the first division in 1926, he lost his place between the posts to Harry Wilkes. During the Christmas period of 1927, Villa were beaten 5–0 at the Baseball Ground and this prompted the club to look for a new goalkeeper to replace Tommy Jackson. The following day, the Rams won 1–0 at Villa Park and on 28 December Villa signed Olney from County's reserve side. Four months after making his Villa debut, he was capped by England, playing in the matches against France and Belgium, which England won 5–1 and 3–1 respectively. In the summer of 1930 he moved to non-league Bilston United, later being appointed manager before returning to league circles with Walsall and Shrewsbury Town.

OLNEY, IAN. An England Under-21 international, Ian Olney won a regular place in the Villa line-up in the 1989–90 season, finishing the campaign second in the scoring list with nine goals. However, the following season he found it difficult to hold down a first-team place. In 1991-92, Ron Atkinson's first season in charge, after appearing in only 14 matches he was allowed to join Oldham Athletic. He cost the Latics £700,000, which is still a club record transfer fee.

OVERSEAS PLAYERS. The club have boasted a number of continental players. French international Didier Six played in 18 league and Cup games during 1984–85, Graham Turner's first season in charge. Defender Kent Neilsen joined Villa from Brondby for £500,000 and made 11 appearances for Denmark during his stay with the club. Polish international full-back Dariusz Kubicki joined the club from Legia Warsaw and made 23 appearances. The Germans Stefan Beinlich and Matthias Breikreuts joined Villa from Bergmann Berlin but were only fringe players and left the club at the end of the 1993–94 season. Partizan Belgrade striker Savo Milosevic joined Villa for a fee of £3.5 million in the 1995 close season and a year later was joined by another former Partizan player, Sasa Curcic, who cost the club a record £4 million from Bolton Wanderers. Villa have three other overseas players on their books: Australian international goalkeeper, Mark Bosnich, Portuguese Fernando Nelson and Trinidad and Tobago star, Dwight Yorke.

OWN GOALS. Gershom Cox of Aston Villa had the misfortune to score the first own goal in the Football League when playing against Wolverhampton Wanderers on the opening day of the first competition on 8 September 1888. On 17 October 1925, Villa were leading Birmingham City 3–0 with just ten minutes to play. Thousands had already started to drift homewards when City's Joe Bradford struck two goals in quick succession to set up an exciting finish. With just seconds remaining, Cyril Spiers the Villa goalkeeper in attempting to clear an attack, managed to throw the ball into his own net for the equaliser. When Aston Villa met Leicester City at Filbert Street on 20 March 1976, the final score was 2–2: quite unremarkable except for the fact that all four goals were scored by Villa's Chris Nicholl. He headed two goals for his own team and kicked in two for his opponents.

P

PACE, DEREK. Scoring on his Villa debut against Burnley in a 3–2 win on 17 March 1951, Derek Pace spent eight seasons at Villa Park without really establishing himself in the first team. Only occasionally did he show his goalscoring ability and on 14 April 1956, he hit a hat-trick in a 3–2 win over Sheffield United, the club Pace was to make his name with. He was 12th man when Villa won the FA Cup in 1957. After scoring three goals in 12 games the following season, he put pen to paper on Boxing Day 1957 and signed for Sheffield United. At Bramall Lane, he scored over 150 goals in 275 first-team outings, helping the Blades gain promotion to the first division in 1961. He had a short spell with Notts County before ending his league career with Walsall.

PARKER, GARRY. Unable to win a regular place in Luton Town's midfield, Garry Parker joined Hull City, where he missed very few games in his two years with the second division club. It was while he was at Boothferry Park that he won the first of his six England Under-21 caps and attracted the attention of the bigger clubs. He signed for Nottingham Forest in March 1988 and won two League Cup winners' medals and an FA Cup runners-up medal in his time at the City Ground. After playing in 151 first-team games for Forest, he joined Villa in November 1991 for £650,000. Although he immediately became a regular first choice in Villa's midfield, he had a quiet first season before having an outstanding one in 1992–93 as Villa finished runners-up in the Premier League. A great striker of the ball, many of his goals have been of the spectacular variety. He had played in 99 league and Cup games for Villa when in February 1995 he joined Leicester City, helping them into the Premier League via the play-offs.

PARKES, HARRY. Signing for Villa just before the outbreak of the Second World War, Harry Parkes guested for Northampton Town and West Bromwich Albion during the hostilities as well as scoring 42 goals in 144 outings for Villa and winning a League Cup (North) medal. After making 26 appearances in 1946–47, the first season after the war, Parkes missed just nine games in the following six seasons. He played in all ten outfield positions for the club, but was at his best when playing full-back. That first season, he was so impressive that he was in line for full international honours but a bad arm injury incurred during the match against Derby County cost him his place. He went on to play for Villa until October 1954, retiring at the end of the season after 345 first-team appearances.

PENALTIES. When Aston Villa played at Stoke on 12 September 1892. They were leading 1–0 when the home side were awarded a penalty with just two minutes left. The Villa keeper, Dunning, promptly picked up the ball and booted it out of the ground. By the time it had been recovered, the referee had blown for full-time. Needless to say, after that the rule was amended to allow time to be added on for taking a penalty. Billy Walker scored a hat-trick of penalties for Villa in their 7–1 home win over Bradford City on 12 November 1921. Eric Houghton, who was one of the game's most notable penalty-takers, scoring 17 for Villa, missed one on his debut against Leeds United on 4 January 1930, the Yorkshire side winning 4–3. Goalkeeper Tommy Jackson saved nine penalties during his Villa career, while Joe Rutherford experienced both the highs and lows of facing a penalty. In 1947, he was the Villa hero, saving two penalties in a game against Everton, but three years later he was on the receiving end of Charlie Mitten's hat-trick of penalties, as Manchester United beat Villa 7–0. Villa's Ray Graydon is one of three players to fail from the penalty spot in a Football League

Cup final. He missed against Norwich City in 1975, but Villa still won 1–0.

PFA AWARDS. The Professional Footballers Association award for Player of the Year has gone to three Aston Villa players:
1977 Andy Gray 1990 David Platt 1993 Paul McGrath
The Young Player of the Year award has gone to two Aston Villa players:
1977 Andy Gray 1981 Gary Shaw

PHILLIPS, CHARLIE. A Welsh schoolboy international, Charlie Phillips signed professional forms for Wolverhampton Wanderers and in six and a half seasons at Molineux, scored 70 goals in 248 senior games. He won the first of his 13 full caps for Wales during his time at Wolverhampton and his last three whilst with Villa following his £9,000 transfer in January 1936. He scored Villa's opening goal on his debut in a 3–1 win at Derby County on 1 February 1936 but his career at Villa Park was hampered by injuries and in just over two years, he played in only 22 first-team games. In his last season at the club, he helped Villa win the second division championship, before moving to St Andrews to end his career with Birmingham.

PHILLIPS, LEIGHTON. Capped by Wales 58 times, Leighton Phillips made 180 league appearances for Cardiff City before joining Aston Villa in September 1974 for £100,000. Making his debut as a substitute in a 3–0 win over Millwall, he helped Villa to win promotion in his first season at the club. He won a League Cup winners' tankard in 1977 as Villa beat Everton, but the following year the versatile performer who played in 175 games for Villa was sold to Swansea City. After three years at the Vetch Field in which

Leighton Phillips

he helped the Swans win promotion twice, he had a short spell with Charlton Athletic before ending his career as a non-contract player with Exeter City.

PITCH. The Villa Park pitch measures 115 yards x 75 yards.

PLASTIC. Four Football League clubs have replaced their normal grass playing pitches with artificial surfaces at one stage or another. Queens Park Rangers were the first in 1981 but the Loftus Road artificial pitch was discarded in 1988 in favour of a return to turf. Luton Town, Oldham Athletic and Preston North End are the other three clubs. Villa never played on Preston North End's plastic, but won 1–0 at Boundary Park in 1987–88 thanks to an Alan McInally goal. They visited Oldham again in the sixth round of the FA Cup but went down 3-0. Villa have played on the Loftus Road plastic on six occasions in all competitions, losing five. Their only success came on 17 December 1985 when an Alan Birch goal separated the teams. After five defeats at Kenilworth Road, Villa got their first point in 1988–89 in a 1–1 draw after a Johnson own goal. The following season, they won 1–0 with Derek Mountfield netting for Villa.

PLATT, DAVID. Though he signed professional forms for Manchester United, David Platt never made the first-team and was allowed to join Crewe Alexandra on a free transfer. At Gresty Road, he made rapid progress and after scoring 61 goals in 152 first-team appearances moved to Aston Villa for £200,000 in January 1988. He made his debut in a 3–2 defeat at Blackburn Rovers, scoring one of Villa's goals. In fact, he scored in his first three games for the club and proved to be a regular marksman from midfield in his three and a half years with the club. He was top scorer in seasons 1989–90 and 1990–91 with 24 goals in each campaign. Platt won his first international cap against Italy in 1989–90, coming on as a substitute, but after impressing for England in the World Cup finals of 1990, he became the target for a number of top European clubs. At the end of the 1990–91 season, after he had scored 68 goals in 155 appearances, he left Villa for the Italian *Serie A* club, Bari, in a £5.5 million transfer deal. He had a disappointing first season with the Italian club for they were relegated and he left to play for Juventus and later

Sampdoria. The midfield dynamo was still an important member of the England team and after captaining them in Euro '96 had 62 caps to his name. He returned to England in the summer of 1995 to play for Arsenal but picked up a knee injury that meant he wasn't fully fit until the later stages of the season.

PLAYERS UNION. The Players Union was formed in 1907. It was unable to make any progress in the retain and transfer system though slowly growing in both size and influence. During the 1911–12 season, the union took the test case of Villa's Kingaby and his dispute with the club to the King's Bench division, but the judge ruled in favour of the club. Yet Kingaby had a strong case, for Villa had put a ridiculously high sum on his head, which had virtually kept him out of the game for almost two years. The Players Union's lawyers based much of their case on the club's motives, accusing them of malice, rather than the system itself. The defeat was a great political setback for the union. The Players Union eventually became known as the Professional Footballers Association.

POINTS. Under the three points for a win system which was introduced in 1981–82, Aston Villa's best points tally was the 78 points gained in 1987–88 when the club finished runners-up in the second division. However, the club's best points haul under the old two points for a win system was 70 points in 1971–72 when they won the third division championship. This would have netted them 102 points under the present system. Villa's worst record under either system was the meagre 18 points secured in 1890–91 when the club played only 22 games. Under a 42-match programme, Villa's lowest points total is 29 in seasons 1966–67 and 1969–70 when the club were relegated from the first and second divisions respectively.

POSTPONED. The Bristol City v Aston Villa FA Cup tie, played at the second attempt on 16 January 1963, which finished 1–1, had its replay postponed 11 times before Villa with goals from Burrows, Baker and Thomson won 3–2 on 7 March 1963.

POTTS, VIC. Though he was born in Aston, Vic Potts slipped through the club's net, joining Tottenham Hotspur in 1934.

Despite impressing other clubs when he played for Spurs' junior team, Northfleet United, he was released and allowed to join Doncaster Rovers. He had one season at Belle Vue before the outbreak of the Second World War brought him back to the Midlands to work on aircraft generators. He soon began guesting for Villa and in 1944 won a League Cup (North) winners' tankard. One of the game's fastest full-backs, he made his league debut in the 1–0 defeat at Middlesbrough in the opening game of the 1946–47 season and went on to play in 72 league and Cup games before knee trouble forced him to retire from playing. Potts then joined Eric Houghton as second-team trainer at Notts County before joining Walsall in a similar capacity eight years later. In 1963, his career went full circle when he joined Spurs as a scout.

POWELL, IVOR. Turning professional in 1937, Ivor Powell made his league debut for Queens Park Rangers during the 1938–39 season and after playing throughout the war years, took his tally of league games for the Loftus Road club to 112 before joining Aston Villa in December 1948. A Welsh international, Powell won four of his eight caps whilst with Villa and after making his debut in a 1–1 draw at Anfield, he played in 82 consecutive league and Cup games before injury ruled him out in October 1950. An ever-present in 1949–50, he moved to Port Vale in the summer of 1951, becoming player-manager of Bradford City the following year.

PREMIER LEAGUE. After a modest start to the Premier League's inaugural season of 1992–93, Villa's impressive side, managed by the garrulous Ron Atkinson, almost won the title. There was a tense run-in with Manchester United to determine the fate of the championship but United, who had fallen away, produced the results when it mattered and Villa, who cracked under pressure over the last ten games or so, had to be content with second place. Though Ron Atkinson spent heavily in the close season to bring Andy Townsend and Guy Whittingham to Villa Park, the 1993–94 season was only mediocre with far too many draws and as many defeats as wins. The 1994–95 season was a controversial one for Villa as they only just guaranteed their place in the Premiership with a point at already doomed Norwich City on the last day of the campaign. Yet, during the season, Villa thrashed

Wimbledon 7–1 with Tommy Johnson grabbing a hat-trick in the club's biggest win for 33 years. The following season Villa won three of their opening four games, their best start to a league campaign since 1980. Second was the highest place they reached and they ended the season in fourth place where they had been since early February – an improvement on their fortunes over the previous two seasons. In 1996–97, Villa ended the season in fifth place to qualify for a place in the following season's UEFA Cup competition.

PROMOTION. Aston Villa have been promoted on five occasions. The first time was in 1937–38 after relegation two years earlier. Villa won the second division championship, finishing four points clear of Manchester United. Relegated to the second division in 1958–59 after 14 seasons of top-flight football, Villa bounced back immediately, winning the second division championship at the first time of asking. During the season they beat Charlton Athletic 11–1 with Gerry Hitchens scoring five of the goals. Villa won promotion for a third time in 1971–72 following relegation to the third division for the first time in their history in 1969-70. After a good start, they made certain of promotion with 15 victories from 18 matches between 13 November 1971 and 15 March 1972. They finished five points in front of Brighton and Hove Albion. In 1974–75 Villa returned to the first division after finishing as runners-up to Manchester United. Promotion was clinched by the club taking full points from the last eight fixtures. The club last won promotion in 1987–88. Though they recorded only one victory in the first seven games, a 12 match unbeaten run put Villa top of the table by the turn of the year. They lost seven out of ten games towards the end of the season but rallied to finish as runners-up to Millwall. Their 1–1 draw at Swindon Town on the last day of the season only proved good enough because Villa's rivals, Bradford City and Middlesbrough, both lost.

Q

QUICKEST GOAL. On 3 December 1938, Bob Iverson, playing at left-half against Charlton Athletic at Villa Park, achieved the feat of scoring a goal 9.6 seconds from the kick-off, then a British record. Villa went on to win 2–0 with O'Donnell grabbing the other goal. Villa's Bob Chatt is on record as having scored the fastest goal in an FA Cup final, when he scored after just 39 seconds. It was the only goal of the game, giving Villa victory over West Bromwich Albion at the Crystal Palace in 1895.

R

RAMSAY, GEORGE. Signed in 1876, George Ramsay was an important member of the Villa team, captaining them to their first trophy success in 1880 when they won the Birmingham Cup. As a youngster, he had learned his football in the cobbled streets of the Cathcart district of Glasgow, but none of the major Scottish clubs were prepared to take him on. Their loss was Villa's gain as the popular Scot, clad in a small polo cap and long pants, became a great favourite with the home supporters. Unfortunately in 1882 his career was cut short by injury and two years later he became Villa's secretary, a position he held until 1926. During that time, the club won the FA Cup and the league championship six times each. Together with John Lindsay, he discovered the Perry Barr ground in Wellington Road and in 1896 he helped Fred Rinder negotiate the purchase of Villa Park. He acted as honorary adviser and was the club's vice-president until his death at Llandrindod Wells in October 1935, thus ending 59 years of loyal service to Aston Villa.

RAPID SCORING. When Villa beat Burnley 10–0 on the opening day of the 1925–26 season, they took the lead after just 20 seconds when Len Capewell shot home from fully 20 yards. The Villans led 4–0 at half-time, but in the second half they completely demolished the Turf Moor side and should have scored at least ten more goals. As it was, they scored six in the space of 33 minutes in that second period, with Capewell scoring five, Walker three and York and Stephenson one apiece.

RECEIPTS. The club's record receipts are £1,005,402 for the Manchester United v Crystal Palace FA Cup semi-final played at Villa Park on 9 April 1995.

RELEGATION. Aston Villa have been relegated on only five occasions. Their first taste came in 1935–36 when, after conceding 110 goals, they went down to the second division for the first time in their history. Middlesbrough, West Bromwich Albion and Arsenal had all scored seven goals at Villa Park. Villa spent only two seasons in the second division before winning promotion. They were next relegated in 1958–59 when they conceded the only goal of the match against West Bromwich Albion in the last minute of the last match of the season. The club were relegated for a third time in 1966–67. Then in 1969–70 Villa slipped into the third division for the first time in their history. Bruce Rioch who played in every game that season, was the club's top scorer with just six goals. Villa's fifth and final experience of relegation came in 1986–87. They were never out of the first division relegation zone and ended the season bottom of the league. However, as in 1959–60, the club won promotion after just one season out of the top flight.

REYNOLDS, JACK. Jack 'Baldy' Reynolds played in five international matches for Ireland but, when it came to light that he was born in Blackburn, he was capped eight times for England and was selected for the Football League. He had spent most of his youth in Ireland, but in 1884 he returned to live in Blackburn, only to be posted back to the Emerald Isle with the East Lancashire Regiment two years later. Playing first for Distillery and then Ulster, he joined West Bromwich Albion in March 1892 and a month later scored against Villa in the FA Cup final. He signed for Villa in May 1893 and added two more FA Cup winners' medals to his collection and two league championship medals. He left Villa after the double season of 1896–97, moving to Celtic and helping them win the Scottish League in his first season.

Kevin Richardson

RICHARDSON, KEVIN. After making his debut for Everton in November 1981, he appeared the following season in both the League Cup and FA Cup finals for the Toffees. He won a league championship medal in 1984–85 but at the beginning of the 1986–87 season he joined Watford. An influential member of the Vicarage Road club's side, he was instrumental in Watford's 3–1 FA Cup sixth-round victory over Arsenal, prompting the Gunners to sign him in August 1987. A versatile player, he won another league championship medal in 1988–89 but at the end of the following season, after a bad injury, he signed for Spanish team Real Sociedad of San Sebastian, linking up with John Aldridge and Dalian

Atkinson. In August 1991, he joined Atkinson at Villa Park and played in every one of Villa's 51 games without once being substituted. As team captain, he was ever present again the following season and played in 102 consecutive league games before missing a match. He played in 170 league and Cup games for Villa before joining Coventry City for £300,000 in February 1995.

RIMMER, JIMMY. Born at Southport, goalkeeper Jimmy Rimmer graduated through Manchester United's junior teams, winning an FA Youth Cup winners' medal in 1964. After making his first-team debut for United on their 1967 tour of Australia, he spent much of his time as understudy to Alex Stepney before being loaned to Swansea City in October 1973. Harry Gregg, the former United and Ireland keeper, was the manager at Vetch Field and he improved Jimmy Rimmer's game before returning him to Old Trafford. Rimmer joined

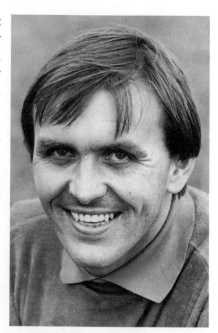

Jimmy Rimmer

Arsenal in March 1974 and won an England cap against Italy in New York in 1976. He made 120 league appearances for the Gunners but after a long drawn out dispute with manager Terry Neill, he signed for Aston Villa. He won league championship, European Cup and European Super Cup medals with Villa before leaving to join Swansea in August 1983. A consistent and agile goalkeeper, Jimmy Rimmer had appeared in 285 first-team games for Villa.

RINDER, FRED. Liverpudlian Fred Rinder joined Villa's committee in 1887 and five years later saved the club from financial ruin. He called a special members' meeting after which he was installed as the club's financial secretary. One of his first moves was to erect turnstiles at the Wellington Road ground in Perry Barr, thus smashing a ticket racket and more than trebling gate receipts. He also introduced other good business practices and over the next ten years showed the way forward, as Villa won five league championships and the FA Cup twice. Just before the First World War, he unveiled his plans for a Villa Park holding somewhere in the region of 120,000. But after the building of the Trinity Road Stand, the club were around £55,000 in debt and after 38 years at Villa Park, he resigned. He returned to the club in 1936 and, though he was then 82 years old, he still had great plans for the Villa Park ground. He did not see the next phase completed, for in January 1939, the man who created Villa Park died. His funeral in Birmingham was attended by 300 mourners, many of whom were leading figures in the game of football.

RIOCH, BRUCE. Bruce Rioch shot to prominence during the 1967–68 season, when he scored 24 goals in 44 league appearances for Luton Town as the Hatters won the fourth division championship. In July 1969, Villa manager Tommy Docherty brought Bruce and his brother Neil to Villa Park in a combined £100,000 deal. In 1971, Bruce Rioch collected a runners-up award in the League Cup final and in 1972 won a third division championship medal. His form for Villa was outstanding, yet in February 1974, a £200,000 offer from Derby County took him to the Baseball Ground. In his first full season with the Rams, he won a league championship medal and was an ever-present. In October 1976, Rioch, not a prolific scorer, hit four goals for Derby against Spurs. Two months later, he was on his way to Goodison Park for £180,000 but within a year he was back with Derby County for £150,000. Though born in Aldershot, he qualified to play for Scotland through his parents and in the 1978 World Cup became the only English-born player to captain Scotland in a full international. Unfortunately, his international career ended after Scotland's poor performance in those finals in Argentina. He had won 24 caps. In March 1980, he was released by Derby and joined Seattle Sounders in the NASL, alternating with the position of player-coach at Torquay United. In 1982, he took over at Middlesbrough, taking them from the brink of liquidation to promotion from the third division in

1986–87 and then into the first division via the play-offs the following season. They were relegated after their first season in the top flight and Rioch was sacked. He had a spell managing Millwall before taking Bolton Wanderers into the Premiership two seasons after gaining promotion from the second division. He then left to take over at Arsenal but lost his job early in the 1996–97 season and is now Stewart Houston's assistant at Queens Park Rangers.

ROBSON, JOHN. Born in Consett, John Robson began his league career with Derby County where he won seven England Under-23 caps and appeared for the Football League. He played in 172 league games for the Rams and was well on his way to winning a league championship medal when Vic Crowe persuaded him to join Villa in December 1972 for a fee of £90,000. Making his Villa debut at full-back against Sheffield Wednesday, he later appeared in midfield following John Gidman's meteoric rise. Robson won a League Cup winners' medal in 1975 and played an important role in helping the club win promotion from the second division. He had appeared in 176 league and Cup games for Villa when he was sadly forced to leave the game suffering from multiple sclerosis. The club staged a testimonial match for the popular player in October 1978 with a Select International XI providing the opposition.

ROSS, IAN. Glasgow-born Ian Ross assumed the role of utility man at Anfield, where he began his league career, until manager Bill Shankly began to employ his tenacious qualities to shackle specific opponents. Also able to use the ball constructively, he would have been guaranteed a first-team place at most clubs, but not at Liverpool and in February 1972 he joined Villa for £70,000. He captained Villa to League Cup success and promotion in 1975 after helping the club win the third division championship three years earlier. He played in 204 first-team games for Villa before joining Peterborough United in 1976. He later had spells coaching Wolves and Villa before working abroad in a similar capacity in the Middle East, South Africa and Australia. Returning to England in 1982, he played as a non-contract player with Hereford United before being appointed manager-coach at Icelandic side FC Valur. In 1992, he was appointed manager of

Huddersfield Town and led the side to the third division play-offs – yet at the end of the following season, he was sacked.

RUGBY UNION. In 1908–09, Villa Park was one of the venues chosen for a rugby international between England and the touring Australians. The New Zealand All-Blacks have also played at Villa Park, beating a North Midlands XV in October 1924. Twenty-seven years later, R.I. Scorer's XV played the North Midlands Select in front of a crowd of just over 12,000.

RUMBELOWS CUP. see Football League Cup.

RUNNERS-UP. Aston Villa have been first division runners-up on nine occasions including their first season in the Football League, 1888–89, when Preston North End won the championship.

RUTHERFORD, JOE. Goalkeeper Joe Rutherford began his career with Southport and played in 88 league games for the Haig Avenue side before signing for Villa in 1939. He made his debut in a 5–1 win over Birmingham City on 4 March that year and played in 11 games before war interrupted his career. During the hostilities, Rutherford guested for Nottingham Forest but when league football resumed in 1946–47, he was Villa's first-choice keeper. He missed just one match in that first season after the war and was the Villa goalkeeper when Manchester United's Charlie Mitten scored a hat-trick of penalties in the Reds' 7–0 win in March 1950. He played in 156 league and Cup games for Villa before leaving the game in the autumn of 1951. He later helped Eric Houghton to run the club's Pools Department and in 1979 he was asked to look after Bodymoor Heath, the club's training ground.

S

SAUNDERS, DEAN. The son of Roy who played for Liverpool and Swansea City, Dean Saunders made his league debut for Swansea City but was not highly thought of by manager John Bond. Following a loan spell at Cardiff City, he signed for Brighton and Hove Albion. Scoring 15 goals in 1985–86, his first season for the Seagulls, he made his international debut for Wales against the Republic of Ireland in March of that campaign. Towards the end of the following season, he joined Oxford United but at

Dean Saunders

the end of the 1987–88 season they were relegated to the second division and he was sold to Derby County. In three seasons at the Baseball Ground, he was the Rams leading scorer, including 17 goals from a total of 37 scored in 1990–91. During the close season he moved to Liverpool for £2.9 million, a record transfer fee between two English clubs. Despite finishing as leading scorer in all competitions and collecting an FA Cup winners' medal, he made just six appearances in 1992–93 before joining Aston Villa for £2.3 million. He made his debut at Leeds United in September and played in every other game that season, finishing as leading goalscorer with 17 goals as Villa ended the season in second place, ten points adrift of Manchester United. He was top scorer in 1993–94 with ten goals, including a hat-trick against Swindon Town, and in 1994–95 with 15 goals. At the end of that season, he joined Turkish club Galatasaray before returning to the Premiership with Nottingham Forest.

SAUNDERS, RON. A bustling, all-action centre-forward, Ron Saunders made his League debut for Everton in 1951, but after only three appearances, he moved to non-league Tonbridge. His league career was resurrected by Gillingham who signed him in May 1957. Portsmouth saw his potential and he went on to make 258 league and Cup appearances for Pompey, scoring 156 goals before later playing for Watford and Charlton Athletic. Saunders started on the road to management with Southern League Yeovil Town in 1968

Ron Saunders

but after twelve months joined Oxford United. Obviously impressed with his work at the Manor Ground, Norwich City offered him their manager's post in 1969. After taking the Canaries to the second division championship in 1971–72 and to the final of the League Cup, he resigned after a poor start to the 1973–74 season. He had five months in charge at Manchester City before joining Villa in June 1974. Saunders transformed a rather disappointing Villa side into League Cup winners and runners-up in the second division in his first season in charge and was named Manager of the Year. In 1980–81, Villa won their first league championship since 1910. It was an outstanding achievement by Saunders and qualified the club for the following season's European Cup. They had reached the quarter-finals when Saunders surprisingly resigned to become manager of Birmingham City. He helped the Blues to win promotion from the second division in 1985 before joining West Bromwich Albion as manager in February 1986. He failed to prevent the Baggies from being relegated and was sacked in September 1987.

SAWARD, PAT. Born in London of Irish parents, Pat Saward was brought up in County Cork before returning to these shores as a 15-year-old. After playing as an amateur with Crystal Palace, he signed professional forms for Millwall and played in 118 league games for the Lions before joining Villa in the summer of 1955 for £10,000. After making his debut at inside-left, he moved to left-half where his stirring performances helped bring the FA Cup to Villa Park in 1957 and win the second division championship in 1960. He won 18 caps for the Republic of Ireland, 13 of them during his six seasons with Villa. Joining Huddersfield Town in 1961, he played in 59 league games for the Leeds Road club before being appointed player-coach of Coventry City. In 1970 he joined Brighton and Hove Albion as manager, steering them into the second division before ending his involvement with football by coaching the Saudi Arabian club, Al-Nasr.

SCORES – HIGHEST. Aston Villa's highest score in any first-team match was their 19–2 win over RAF (Lichfield) on 28 March 1942 when they won the Birmingham and District League. The club's best victory in the FA Cup is 13–0 over Wednesbury Old Athletic in a first-round match on 3 October 1886. In the Football League, Accrington were beaten 12–2 in a first division match on 12 March 1892 and Charlton Athletic 11–1 in a second division match on 24 November 1959.

SECOND DIVISION. Aston Villa have had five spells in the second division. The first followed their relegation from division one in 1935–36. After finishing ninth in their first season of division two football, Villa bounced back into the top flight by winning the second division championship in 1937–38, four points ahead of second-placed Manchester United. Villa had 14 seasons of first division football before being relegated to the second division a second time in 1958–59. However, this time Villa needed only one season in Division Two as they won the championship in fine style, including beating Charlton Athletic 11–1. Relegated in 1966–67, Villa spent three seasons in the second division before dropping down to the third division for the first time in their history. The club played third division football for two seasons before winning the title and returning for a fourth spell in Division Two. This time it took Villa three seasons to achieve promotion to the first division by finishing second to Manchester United. Villa had 12 seasons in the first division, winning the league title in 1980–81 before being relegated six seasons later. This spell in the second division lasted for just one season, 1987–88, and they returned to the top flight as runners-up to Millwall.

SEMI-FINALS. Up to the end of the 1996–97 season, Aston Villa had been involved in 18 FA Cup semi-finals and ten Football League Cup semi-finals.

SEWELL, JACKIE. A prolific goalscorer, Jackie Sewell began his footballing career with Notts County, whom he helped win the third division (South) title in 1949–50. Forming a deadly striking partnership with Tommy Lawton, he scored 97 goals in 179 league games for the Meadow Lane club. When he was transferred to Sheffield Wednesday in March 1951 for £34,500, he became the most expensive footballer in Britain. He played in 175 games for the Owls, scoring 92 goals and in his four years at Hillsborough, he gained six England caps. In 1954, he scored a hat-trick for the Football League against the League of Ireland at Maine Road. He joined Aston Villa in December 1955 for a fee of £20,000, scoring on his debut in a 2–2 draw at Sheffield United. Though not quite matching his strike rate with his previous two clubs, he went on to score 40 goals in 144 outings and won an FA Cup winners' medal in 1957. He later played for Hull City before coaching in Rhodesia (Zimbabwe), Zambia and the Belgian Congo (Zaire.)

SHAW, GARY. The only Birmingham-born player in Villa's league championship and European Cup-winning teams of 1981 and 1982, Gary Shaw made his debut coming on as a substitute at Bristol City in August 1978. The Ashton Gate ground was also the venue for his first league hat-trick in December 1979 as Villa won 3–1. During Villa's Championship-winning season of 1980–81, Shaw won the first of seven Under-21 caps for England when he played against the Republic of Ireland. Developing a terrific understanding with Peter Withe, he scored 18 League goals in 40 appearances. When Villa won the European Cup in 1981–82, Shaw was voted by the European Football Writers' Association the Top Player in the European Competition. A regular in the Villa side until the end of the following season, Shaw was then struck down by a series of niggling injuries and after going on loan to Blackpool, he left Villa Park in the summer of 1988, having played in 212 first-team matches, scoring 80 goals. He later played for BK Copenhagen of Denmark and FC Klagenfurt of Austria before returning to these shores to play for Walsall and Shrewsbury Town.

SHELL, FRANK. In December 1937, in only his second game for Villa, Frank Shell scored a hat-trick as Stockport County were beaten 7–1. Forming a good understanding with Frank Broome, Shell helped Villa to the second division championship that season and to the semi-final of the FA Cup. Though he played in only a handful of matches the following season, he added a few more during the Second World War as well as guesting for Northampton Town and Walsall. He returned to Villa Park after the hostilities but was immediately transferred to Birmingham City, later playing for Hereford United and Mansfield Town.

SIMOD CUP. The Simod Cup replaced the Full Members' Cup from the 1987–88 season for two seasons. Villa's first-round match that season saw them crash out to Bradford City, beaten 5–0 at Villa Park in a dreadfully one-sided contest. In 1988–89, Villa made amends, defeating Birmingham City 6–0 in front of a first-round crowd of 8,324 but they went down 2–1 at the Baseball Ground in an exciting match in which Alan McInally scored for Villa.

SIMS, NIGEL. Understudy to England goalkeeper Bert Williams at Wolverhampton Wanderers for eight seasons, Nigel Sims played in only 38 league games for the Molineux club before joining Villa in March 1956. Despite weighing over 14 stone, Sims was a most agile keeper and in nine seasons at Villa Park, won an FA Cup winners' medal, a League Cup winners' tankard and a second division championship medal. In 1959, he guested for Arsenal during the Gunners tour of Italy, following a dispute with the Villa board. He appeared in 309 first-team games for Villa before being transferred to Peterborough United in September 1964. He appeared in a further 16 league games for the Posh but within a year he went to play in Canada, returning to England six years later.

SLEEUWENHOEK, JOHN. Born at Wednesfield the son of a Dutch Army paratrooper, John Sleeuwenhoek was taken to Holland by his parents but returned to these shores following the death of his father. An England schoolboy and youth international, he made his Villa debut in a 4–0 win over Bolton Wanderers towards the end of the 1960–61 season. Following Jimmy Dugdale's departure to Queens Park Rangers, Sleeuwenhoek became Villa's first-choice centre-half and in 1962–63 won two England Under-23 caps. In 1966–67 he was ever present and scored the only goal of his Villa career in the 2–1 win over Stoke City. In November 1967, he joined Birmingham City, making 30 league appearances for the Blues before going on loan to Torquay United. He ended his league career with Oldham Athletic in 1972, although he was persuaded to play in the Cheshire County League the following year. Sadly, Sleeuwenhoek died in the summer of 1989, aged 45.

SMALL, BRYAN. Having made his Villa debut at Everton in October 1991, most of Bryan Small's games in that first season were at left-back standing in for Steve Staunton, or in midfield. The following season he became a regular member of the England Under-21 squad and impressed in the 14 games he played for Villa at left-back when Staunton moved into midfield. Injuries hampered his progress and in March 1996 after a loan spell at Birmingham City, he joined Bolton Wanderers on a free transfer. In 1996–97 he helped them return to the Premiership as champions of the first division.

SMART, TOMMY. Standing 6ft 2½ins and weighing 13st 8lbs, Tommy Smart's size used to put fear into the opposition forwards. Beginning his career with Blackheath Town, Smart moved to Halesowen from where he signed for Villa in January 1920. He made his debut in a 2–2 draw against Everton on St Valentine's Day and played in 11 games that season, gaining an FA Cup winners' medal after Villa beat Huddersfield Town in the final at Stamford Bridge. In 1921, he made his international debut for England against Scotland, the first of five caps for his country. He formed an outstanding full-back pairing with Tommy Mort and the two of them, known as Death and Glory were regulars in the Villa side until 1932–33. Tommy Smart went on to play in 452 league and Cup games for Villa, leaving the club in May 1934 to play for Brierley Hill Alliance.

SMITH, LES. Starting his footballing career at Molineux, Les Smith found it hard to win a regular place in the Wolves line-up with Hancocks and Mullen occupying the wing positions. He had scored 15 goals in 88 league appearances in just under ten years when Eric Houghton signed him for Villa. He made his debut at home to Arsenal in February 1956 and was a regular member of the Villa side, winning an FA Cup winners' medal the following season. Smith was forced to quit the game towards the end of the 1958–59 season after rupturing his Achilles tendon at Nottingham Forest, though it was January 1960 before he officially hung up his boots.

SMITH, LESLIE. When he was 17 years old, Leslie Smith played for Wimbledon in the FA Amateur Cup final, collecting a loser's medal against Bishop Auckland in 1935. He had a short spell with Hayes before signing professional forms for Brentford. He played in 62 league games for the Bees before the Second World War and helped them win the London Wartime Cup in 1942. Also during the war, he guested for Chelsea and was in their side when they won the League Cup (South) in 1945. Having played for England against Romania in 1939, he went on to appear in 13 Wartime and Victory internationals, as well as representing the FA and RAF XIs. Smith joined Villa in October 1945 for a fee of £7,500 and scored four goals in eight FA Cup appearances that season. A fast, direct winger, Smith made 107 consecutive league appearances for Villa following his debut in the opening game of the 1946–47 season. After scoring 37 goals in 191 first-team games, he returned to Brentford in the summer of 1952, only for injury to cut short his career.

SMITH, STEVE. Joining Villa in 1893, Steve Smith made his league debut a couple of months later, scoring the first goal in a 4–0 win over Burnley. At the end of that season, he won the first of five league championship medals. He won FA Cup winners' medals in 1895 and 1897 and in the first of those successful Cup campaigns, won his one and only cap for England, scoring in the 3–0 win over Scotland at Goodison Park. Playing most of his games on the left wing, Smith's best season was 1894–95 when he scored 18 league and Cup goals, including a hat-trick in a 3–1 win at Blackburn Rovers. He suffered on occasions with niggling injuries and his absence from the team often coincided with a Villa defeat. After scoring 42 goals in 191 games, he left Villa Park for Portsmouth in 1901, where he helped the club win the Southern League title in his first season. He later became player-manager of New Brompton (Gillingham) before leaving the game two years later.

SOUTHGATE, GARETH. Starting his career with Crystal Palace, Gareth Southgate was the only ever-present in 1994–95 when the Eagles were relegated to the first division. As the Palace captain, he led by example right up to the final whistle of the last match of that campaign. During the summer of 1995, Southgate, who had played in 191 first-team games for Palace, joined Villa in a £2.5 million deal. Though he arrived at Villa Park as a midfield player, he joined Ehiogu and McGrath in a three-man defensive system. A hard-working player with two good feet, he was able to bring the ball out of defence and distribute it effectively. He fully justified his fee and after making his international debut as a substitute against Portugal in December 1995, he forced his way into England's Euro '96 squad. Despite his penalty shoot-out miss, Southgate was one of the stars of an England team that reached the semi-finals of the competition.

SPENCER, HOWARD. Howard Spencer began a 42-year association with Villa in 1894, following up a successful playing career by serving on the board of directors from 1909 to 1936. Making his debut against West Bromwich Albion on 13 October 1894, he went on to play in 294 games for Villa, winning four league championship and two FA Cup winners' medals and captaining the 1905 Cup-winning side. Spencer was known as The Prince of Full-backs and also as Gentle Howard, a reflection of the fairness that was a feature of his play. He appeared in six internationals for England and made nine appearances for the Football League, these being considered modest recognition for a player who was widely acknowledged and admired for his skills.

SPINK, NIGEL. Goalkeeper Nigel Spink joined Aston Villa from his local club Chelmsford City in January 1977, but had to wait nearly three years before making his debut at Nottingham Forest on Boxing Day 1979. Remarkably, his next first-team appearance was in the 1982 European Cup final against Bayern Munich in Rotterdam. He had been named as substitute that evening but had to replace Jimmy Rimmer who damaged his neck after only eight minutes. Spink played superbly and collected a winners' medal after a Peter Withe goal had given Villa a

Nigel Spink

1–0 win. He eventually replaced Rimmer on a permanent basis midway through the 1982–83 season and at the end of that campaign toured Australia with England, winning his one cap when he replaced Peter Shilton at half-time in a goalless draw. Injuries marred the next few seasons for him but in 1987–88 he was an ever-present as Villa were promoted to the first division. When Villa were first division runners-up to Liverpool in 1989–90 Spink again played in every game, conceding just 38

Simon Stainrod

goals. He lost his first-team place to Les Sealey in 1991 but regained it a year later, playing in every game except one in the 1992–93 season. Eventually losing his place to Mark Bosnich after appearing in 461 first-team games, he joined West Bromwich Albion in January 1996.

SPONSORS. Sponsored by Mita Copiers since the early 1980s, Villa switched to Muller Yogurt before now being sponsored by AST Computers.

STAINROD, SIMON. Despite supporting Sheffield Wednesday as a boy, Simon Stainrod got his start in League football with Sheffield United. He joined Oldham Athletic in March 1979, scoring 21 goals in 69 league appearances for the Boundary Park club before signing for Queens Park Rangers. He scored 48 league goals in 145 appearances for the Loftus Road club including a hat-trick against Sheffield Wednesday, the club he went on to join for a then record fee of £260,000. His stay at Hillsborough was short-lived and in September 1985 he moved to Aston Villa. At Villa Park he often played in a midfield role and scored 16 goals in 63 league games before ending his league career with Stoke City.

STARLING, RONNIE. Born in the north-east, Ronnie Starling went to work down the pit at Unsworth Colliery and then Washington Colliery. In 1924 he attracted the attention of Hull City manager Bill McCracken. The former Newcastle United defender was so anxious to sign Starling, that he gave him a job as an office boy and played him as an amateur. Starling turned professional two years later and after playing in 86 games for the Tigers joined Newcastle United for £3,750. This was the least successful phase of his career and in the summer of 1932 he joined Sheffield Wednesday. In five seasons at Hillsborough, he scored 31 goals in 193 games, captained the club to victory over West Bromwich Albion in the FA Cup final of 1935 and won two caps for England. In January 1937, Starling signed for Aston Villa for a fee of £7,500. Signed by Jimmy Hogan, Starling won a second division championship medal with Villa in 1937–38 and a League Cup (North) tankard in 1944. He remained at Villa Park throughout the war, playing the last of his games against Grimsby Town in April 1947.

STAUNTON, STEVE. Steve Staunton joined Liverpool from the League of Ireland side, Dundalk in August 1986 and was loaned out to Bradford City where he made his Football League debut. It was the 1988–89 season before he played his first game for Liverpool, coming on as substitute against Tottenham Hotspur at Anfield. Eventually displacing David Burrows, he won an FA Cup winners' medal at the end of a season in which he also won his first international cap for the Republic of Ireland. Though he later found it difficult to hold down a regular place in the Anfield side, he played in enough games to win a league championship medal in 1989–90. In 1990–91, he wore six different numbered shirts in making 20 league appearances. In August 1991 he was transferred to Aston Villa for £1.1 million. Making a dream debut, he scored the winning goal in the club's 3–2 win at Sheffield Wednesday on the opening day of the season. An ever-present in 1992–93, he was outstanding in Villa's drive for the Premier League championship. Equally at home at left-back or in midfield, his corners and free kicks are always a threat to the opposition defence. Still a regular for the Republic of Ireland, for whom he has won 62 caps, he has now played in more than 200 first-team games for Villa.

STEPHENSON, CLEM. The eldest of the three Stephenson brothers, Clem signed for Aston Villa in March 1910 but found it tough to break into the side during his early days. He was farmed out to Stourbridge for almost a year, then recalled to Villa Park where he grabbed his opportunity to impress. He showed a sure touch on the ball and was quickly installed as a regular at inside-left, appearing in the 1913 FA Cup final. Guesting for Leeds United during the war, he was back with Villa after the hostilities had ended and appeared in the 1920 FA Cup final against Huddersfield Town, the club he would shortly join. It was in that year that Clem ran into dispute with the Villa board, being suspended along with Frank Barson for failing to turn up for a league game at Bolton. It was a rocky period. Stephenson would not agree to move to the Midlands, continuing to live in the north-east and travelling to Birmingham for match days, totally against Villa's wishes. A transfer was the outcome and in March 1921, after playing in 216 first-team games and scoring 96 goals, he moved to Leeds Road for £3,000. It was the start of a remarkable era for Huddersfield where Stephenson stayed for the next 20 years. He steered his new side to an FA Cup final victory in 1922 – his third winners' medal – skippered them to three consecutive championship victories and during that time won an England cap, against Wales in 1924. Later he turned to management, becoming a proficient and highly respected boss at Leeds Road.

STEPHENSON, GEORGE. George joined his elder brother Clem at Villa Park in November 1919 after the infamous auction of Leeds City players and was also loaned to Stourbridge for a period before finding a regular spot in Villa's line-up during 1925–26 and 1926–27. Having inherited the same family skills, George was a thoughtful and cultured schemer who scored 22 goals for Villa in 95 first-team games spread over seven seasons. He moved to Derby County in November 1927 for £2,000 and scored 56 goals in 121 league and Cup outings for the Rams. He probably displayed his best soccer at the Baseball Ground as Derby challenged strongly for the title. A former junior international, George Stephenson won a place in the England side and actually earned more caps than his famous brother, playing three times for his country between 1927 and 1931. In February 1931 he was off to Hillsborough and a spell with Sheffield Wednesday before switching to Preston North End less than two years later. After he had helped the Deepdale club to promotion, he headed south for Charlton Athletic in 1934. He retired from playing in August 1937 and joined the Valley's training staff before teaming up with his brother Clem at Leeds Road. In August 1947, he was appointed manager of Huddersfield Town in his own right but after several relegation battles, he resigned in March 1952.

SUBSTITUTES. The first-ever Aston Villa substitute was Jimmy MacEwan who came on for Tony Scott against Burnley at Turf Moor on 20 November 1965. The club had to wait until the 25th game of the 1966–67 season for their first goalscoring substitute – Lew Chatterley scored in the 3–2 home win over Blackpool. The greatest number of substitutes used in a single season by Villa under the single substitute rule was 25 in 1968–69. Since 1986–87, two substitutes have been allowed and in 1994–95, 58 were used. The greatest number of substitute appearances for

Villa has been made by Tony Daley who came on during 44 league games and three more times in cup-ties. The most substitute appearances in a season by an individual is ten, a feat Dwight Yorke achieved in both 1990–91 and 1993–94, Graham Fenton in 1994–95 and Ricky Scimeca in 1995–96.

SUSPENSIONS. Jimmy Cowan was suspended by the Villa committee for entering the Powderhall Sprint Handicap in 1896. He entered the event under an assumed name but the Villa officials discovered it. They thought he was at home recovering from an injury. Billy George, one of the finest goalkeepers in England, was suspended by the FA the following year, along with Fred Rinder and George Ramsay. FA rules had been infringed when the club persuaded George to leave the Army. One of the game's greatest centre-halves, Frank Barson, joined Villa from Barnsley. When he refused to move house from Sheffield to Birmingham, he was suspended and then sold to Manchester United for £5,000.

SUSTAINED SCORING. During the 1930–31 season, Villa were battling with Arsenal for the first division title. Tom Waring joined the club from Tranmere Rovers and scored 49 goals in 39 league appearances, setting a new league scoring record for Villa. He scored all four Villa goals on the opening day of the season as they beat Manchester United 4–3 at Old Trafford and scored 13 goals in the first seven games of the season. He went through something of a lean spell in January, scoring only three goals, but recovered his touch the following month with four goals against Sunderland. He needed just one for his 50 league goals in the final match at Hillsborough, but it was not to be and Villa finished the season as runners-up to the Gunners.

SWAIN, KENNY. Starting his league career with Chelsea, Kenny Swain scored 19 goals in 126 outings for the Stamford Bridge club, operating mainly as a striker or in midfield before joining Aston Villa in December 1978. At Villa Park, the Birkenhead-born player was converted into a right-back and won medals for league championship, European Cup and European Super Cup successes in seasons 1980–81 and 1981–82. He made the number two shirt his own following John Gidman's departure for Everton and in the championship-winning season of 1980–81, was an ever-present. He played in 178 first-team games for Villa before moving to Nottingham Forest in 1983. He later helped Portsmouth win promotion to the first division and had a spell on loan at West Bromwich Albion before becoming player-coach at Crewe Alexandra. He appeared in 625 league games for his six clubs before being appointed manager of Wigan Athletic in 1993.

T

TALBOT, ALEC. Alec Talbot joined Villa from Hednesford Town in April 1923, signing professional forms immediately after completing a ten-hour shift down the pit at West Cannock Colliery. Though he played in a 2–0 FA Cup win at Swansea in February 1924, he spent the whole of that season in Villa's Central League team, not gaining a first-team place until 1924–25. An ever-present in seasons 1930–31 and 1931–32, he appeared in 136 consecutive league matches for the club, before playing the last of his 263 league and Cup games at the end of 1934. The following summer, the popular centre-half, nicknamed Tiny joined Bradford Park Avenue but after a short stay, ended his career with Stourbridge.

TALLEST PLAYER. It is impossible to be definite about who was the tallest player ever on Villa's books, as such records are notoriously unreliable. But almost certain to lay claim to the distinction is Ian Ormondroyd at 6ft 5ins. Known as Sticks, he played in 73 first-team games for the club between 1989 and 1991.

TATE, JOE. The youngest of five brothers, Joe Tate joined Villa from Cradley Heath in April 1925. He had to bide his time in the reserves for two and a half years before winning a regular place in the first team, replacing Frank Moss senior when he joined Cardiff City. Tate, originally an inside-left, was switched to left-half with good effect. An ever-present during the 1930–31 season when the club scored 128 goals to finish runners-up in the first division, he held his place until midway through the 1932–33 season, when a series of niggling injuries reduced his appearances. Winning three caps for England, he played his last game for Villa in a 3–2 home defeat by Newcastle United in November 1933. In May 1935, he became player-manager of Brierley Hill but two years later broke his neck in a match against Moor Green and left the game for good.

TAYLOR, DICK. As a player, Dick Taylor was an old-fashioned centre-half who played for Grimsby Town and Scunthorpe United. After retiring, Taylor stayed with the Irons as trainer-coach before linking up with Joe Mercer at Sheffield United. In 1958 he was brought to Villa Park as Mercer's assistant, taking over in 1964 when Mercer left the club. He could not prevent Villa from being relegated in 1966–67 and at the end of that season, he was sacked along with his assistant manager Jimmy Easson and trainer Johnny Dixon.

TAYLOR, GRAHAM. After a playing career with Grimsby Town and Lincoln City, Graham Taylor began his managerial career with Lincoln and in 1976 took them to the Fourth Division title. In June 1977, he received a good offer to take over the reins at Watford. He stayed at Vicarage Road for over ten years, working alongside chairman Elton John. He took Watford from the fourth division to the runners-up spot in the first division in 1983. In 1984, he led them to their first FA Cup final, where they lost to

Graham Taylor

Everton. Deciding he needed a fresh challenge, he became manager of Villa in July 1987. The club were then in the second division and at the end of his first season in charge, they were back in the top flight, after finishing as runners-up to Millwall. After just avoiding relegation in 1988–89, they ended the following campaign as runners-up to Liverpool. Taylor left Villa Park in May 1990 to take over from Bobby Robson as England's team manager. However, his career hit rock bottom with the European Championship of 1992 and within days of England failing to qualify for the 1994 World Cup finals, he had resigned. In April 1994, he was appointed manager of Wolverhampton Wanderers but 20 months later he was replaced by Mark McGhee and returned to Watford as general manager.

TAYLOR, IAN. An industrious goalscoring midfielder, Ian Taylor was Port Vale's leading scorer in 1992–93 with 15 goals and a regular member of the Vale promotion team of 1993–94. He joined Sheffield Wednesday in the close season for £1 million, a fee decided by a tribunal. Six months later, after appearing in just 14 first-team games for the Owls, he joined Aston Villa for another £1 million fee. He marked his Villa debut with a goal in the 3–0 win over Chelsea on 28 December 1994 and played in 22 games during that campaign. He scored the opening goal of Villa's 1995–96 campaign in the 3–1 win over Manchester United on the opening day of the season. A regular performer in the opening half of the season, he suffered from hamstring and ankle injuries before returning to score Villa's second goal in the 3–0 League Cup final win over Leeds United.

TEALE, SHAUN. Southport-born Shaun Teale played for a number of non-league clubs before joining Bournemouth from Weymouth in January 1989. Whilst with Weymouth, he was selected for England against Wales in a semi-professional international in 1988. After making his Bournemouth debut in February 1989, he was an ever-present the following season. Recognised as one of the most accomplished defenders in the lower divisions, he signed for Aston Villa for £300,000 in the summer of 1991. Making his Villa debut against Sheffield Wednesday in the opening game of the 1991–92 season, he went on to be an ever-present. Forming a most effective central defensive partnership with Paul McGrath, he played in 153 first-team games before being allowed to sign for Tranmere Rovers for £500,000 in August 1995. Now playing for Preston North End, he contributed greatly to Villa's outstanding season of 1992–93 when the club only conceded 44 goals in the league.

TELEVISION. Aston Villa's first appearance on BBC's 'Match of the Day' was on 19 December 1964 when they beat Arsenal 3–1 with two goals from Alan Baker and one from Johnny MacLeod. On 22 October 1980 ATV cancelled plans to show highlights of the first division match between Aston Villa and Brighton, when the Seagulls refused to wear shirts that did not carry their sponsor's name. On St Valentine's Day 1988, Villa appeared in the first-ever second division match to be screened live on television. A crowd of 16,957 saw Tony Daley give Villa the lead but their opponents, Middlesbrough, scored twice in the last few minutes to send the majority of the fans packed into Ayresome Park home happy.

TEMPLETON, BOBBY. On leaving school, Bobby Templeton joined his home-town club Kilmarnock before moving to Hibernian, from where he was transferred to Aston Villa in March 1899. Though there is no doubt he was a man of moods, he could certainly rise to the occasion and in 1900 he helped Villa win the league championship, scoring in each of the season's last three matches. A brilliant ball-playing winger, he won the first of his 11 Scottish caps whilst with Villa, playing against England in 1902. One of the game's showmen, he tended to be inconsistent and played in only 71 first-team games in four years at Villa Park. After playing for Villa, he had spells with Newcastle United and Woolwich Arsenal before rejoining Kilmarnock in 1907. After six years north of the border, he moved to Fulham but returned to his beloved Kilmarnock for a third spell before retiring from the game.

THIRD DIVISION. Aston Villa have had just one spell in the third division. Relegated in 1969–70, the club finished fourth in their first season in the division, possibly distracted in their aim for promotion by their appearance in the Football League Cup final at Wembley. However, they achieved their aim in 1971–72, winning the third division championship with a record 70 points. The crowd of 48,110 that went to Villa Park on 12 February 1972 to watch Villa play against Bournemouth was then the highest to watch a division three game in England.

THOMPSON, TOMMY. Tommy Thompson began his career with Newcastle United, making 20 appearances for the Magpies before joining Aston Villa for £12,500 in September 1950. Making his Villa debut at Blackpool that month, Thompson went on to appear in 165 first-team games for the club, scoring 76 goals including three hat-tricks – against Middlesbrough (home 5–3 on 14 November 1953), Manchester City (away 4–2 on 16 October 1954) and Wolverhampton Wanderers (home 4–2 on 12 April 1955). Surprisingly, he was sold to Preston North End for £27,000 in June 1955. During the 1951–52 season, he had won an international call-up, playing for England against Wales, and in April 1957 he won his second cap. At Deepdale, Thompson provided the perfect foil for Tom Finney and scored after only two minutes of his North End debut in a 4–0 win at Everton. He went on to score five times in his first six games for Preston and in 1957–58, he peaked with 34 first division goals as North End finished runners-up to Wolverhampton Wanderers. In a game against Chelsea at Stamford Bridge, Thompson scored a hat-trick for North End but a certain Jimmy Greaves scored all five goals as the home side won 5–4. Thompson scored 117 goals in 188 league games for Preston, before joining Stoke City, where he scored 18 goals in 42 second division matches to help the Potters win promotion. He later ended his career with Barrow before returning to Deepdale to run the junior teams under the managership of Bobby Charlton.

THOMSON, BOBBY. After playing as an amateur with Albion Rovers and Airdrieonians, Bobby Thomson joined Wolverhampton Wanderers in 1953. Competition at Molineux in those days was very tough and in five years Thomson made only one league appearance. In June 1959, he joined Villa and scored on his debut in a 3–0 home win over Sunderland at the end of August. Partnering Jimmy MacEwan on the right, the aggressive Scot scored 20 goals in his 34 league appearances as Villa won the second division championship. The following season, he continued to score goals and hit three in Villa's run to the first-ever League Cup final. They beat Rotherham United over two legs. He played in another League Cup final in 1962–63 and scored Villa's goal as they lost 3–1 over two games to Birmingham City. At the start of the following season he joined the St Andrews club, serving them equally well until in December 1967 he moved to Stockport County, where he ended his career.

TINDALL, MIKE. A star of Villa's youth and Central League sides of the late 1950s, Mike Tindall represented England Youth on eight occasions and in 1958 played in the final of the FIFA Youth Tournament in Luxembourg. However, after making his first-team debut in a 1–1 draw at home to Hull City in December 1959, he failed to establish himself in the Villa side. He had a spell on loan to New York Americans in 1961 and returned a much more competitive player. He had just seemed to turn the corner when, in November 1964, he broke his leg at White Hart Lane. He bounced back and by the time he joined Walsall in the summer of 1968, the popular Tindall had played in 136 league and Cup games for Villa.

TOURS. Though Aston Villa have made many tours, their visit to Germany in May 1938 was a little different. Villa's boss Jimmy Hogan had managed the Austrian national team and so wherever they went they received a warm welcome. They played three matches on the tour and were expected to give the Nazi salute before each game but refused. In the first game, played in 90 degrees of heat, they beat a German Select XI 3–2 in front of a 110,000 crowd. Frank Broome (2) and Frank Shell were Villa's scorers. They won the second game in Stuttgart 2–1 but lost in Dusseldorf in their final match, 1–0.

TOWNSEND, ANDY. Starting his career in non-league football with Welling United and then Weymouth, Andy Townsend joined Southampton in January 1985 but had to wait until the end of the season before making his league debut against Aston Villa. He did not make an immediate impact in the first division and spent the next two seasons alternating between left-back and midfield before establishing himself as a hard-working midfielder in 1987–88. Rather surprisingly, he was sold to Norwich City in

Andy Townsend

the close season and helped the Canaries to fourth place in the top flight, their highest ever league position, and to the semi-finals of the FA Cup. Also whilst at Carrow Road, he won his first international cap, playing for the Republic of Ireland against France in February 1989. Now captain, he has appeared in over 60 internationals for the Republic. After one more season in East Anglia, he joined Chelsea for £1.2 million, immediately displaying the form that made him one of the top midfield operators in the first division. However, when new manager Glenn Hoddle arrived at Stamford Bridge, he saw Townsend as surplus to requirements and in July 1993 he joined Aston Villa for £2.1 million. A creative player, the Maidstone-born midfielder is highly capable of scoring spectacular goals with his left foot, although to date he has only scored eight in Villa's colours in more than 150 league and Cup appearances.

TRANSFERS. The club's record transfer fee received is the £5.5 million that Italian club Bari paid for David Platt in July 1991. During the summer of 1995, Villa spent a total of £9.25 million on three players: £2.5 million on Crystal Palace's Gareth Southgate, £3.25 million on Mark Draper from Leicester City and £3.5 million, the club's then record transfer fee paid, on Partizan Belgrade's Savo Milosevic. The club's record transfer fee was broken in the summer of 1996 when another Serb, Sasa Curcic, was signed from Bolton Wanderers for £4 million. Two days after the 1996–97 season had ended, Villa broke their record transfer fee again when they paid Liverpool £7 million for the services of Stan Collymore.

TURNBULL, FRED. Following a two-month trial in September 1966, Fred Turnbull was taken on as a professional and made his debut the following season in a 1–1 draw at Middlesbrough. In 1970–71, he helped Villa reach the League Cup final – they lost 2–0 to Tottenham Hotspur – and a year later won a third division championship medal, missing just a handful of matches in both seasons. He began to struggle with injuries and in 1974 this big-hearted defender had to retire at the age of 28. In April 1976, he was deservedly granted a testimonial for his loyal service to Aston Villa.

TURNER, GRAHAM. A former England youth international, Graham Turner appeared in 634 league games for Wrexham, Chester and Shrewsbury between 1965 and 1984. He was appointed player-manager of Shrewsbury Town in 1978 and in 1978–9 led them to the third division championship. They also reached the sixth round of the FA Cup that season before losing at Highbury in a replay. In July 1984, he accepted a lucrative offer to take over at Villa Park. However, after two mediocre seasons and a poor start to the 1986–87 campaign, he was sacked. A month later he was offered the manager's job at Wolverhampton Wanderers. After a disappointing start which saw them knocked out of the FA Cup by non-league Chorley, Turner took the club to the fourth division play-offs where they surprisingly lost to Aldershot. However, the following season they won the fourth division championship and the Sherpa Van Trophy final. In 1988–89 they won the third division title in style, but struggled in the second division. In 1994, Graham Turner was replaced by Graham Taylor.

U

UEFA CUP. Villa played their first match in European football on 17 September 1975 when they travelled to the Belgian club Antwerp for the first-round first-leg tie. Ray Graydon scored for Villa but they went down 4–1. Despite applying pressure in the return match at Villa Park, they lost 1–0 and went out at the first hurdle, 5–1 on aggregate. In 1977–78 Villa did much better, reaching the quarter-finals. There were aggregate wins over Fenerbahce (6–0), Gornik Zabrze (3–1) and Atletico Bilbao (3–1) before Villa met Barcelona in the quarter-final. The first leg at Villa Park attracted a crowd of 49,619 and goals from McNaught and Deehan gave Villa a 2–2 draw. Villa fought bravely in the second leg in front of a 90,000 Spanish crowd but despite Brian Little scoring a valuable away goal, they lost 2–1 and crashed out 4–3 on aggregate. After disposing of Vitoria Guimaraes 5–1 on aggregate in the first round of the 1983-84 UEFA Cup, Peter Withe grabbing a second-leg hat-trick, Villa went out in the next round to Spartak Moscow 4–3 on aggregate. They drew the first match in Russia 2–2. In 1990–91, Villa beat Banik Ostrava in the first round of the competition before meeting Italian giants Inter Milan in round two. The first leg at Villa Park was witnessed live by millions of TV viewers and a crowd of 36,461 packed tight inside the ground. Villa dominated the game and won 2–0 with goals from Kent Nielsen and David Platt, but it could have been more. Unfortunately, Villa did not fare as well in the San Siro Stadium and lost 3–0 on a difficult pitch in front of 75,580 partisan fans. In 1993–94, Villa beat Slovan Bratislava 2–1 on aggregate but fell to Deportivo La Coruna in the next round, after having done the hard work with a 1–1 draw in Spain, thanks to a late Dean Saunders goal. But Deportivo came back to win the return at Villa Park 1–0. The following season, Villa beat Inter Milan 4–2 on penalties in a dramatic shoot-out after both sides had won their home match 1–0. A single goal by Turkish side Trabzonspor led to an away-goals defeat in the second round. In 1996–97, Villa went out at the first hurdle, again on the away goals ruling. After drawing the first leg 1–1 at Villa Park against Helsingborgs IF, a goalless second leg ended Villa's interest in the competition.

UNDEFEATED. Aston Villa have remained undefeated at home throughout three League seasons: 1895–96, 1898–99 and 1909–10. The club's best and longest undefeated sequence in the Football League is 37 matches between 24 April 1909 and 22 April 1911. Villa's longest run of undefeated Football League matches home and away is 15, a run they have achieved on the following three occasions: 16 January 1897 to 18 September 1897; 18 December 1890 to 26 March 1891 and from 12 March 1949 to 27 August 1949.

UTILITY PLAYERS. A utility player is one of those particularly gifted footballers who can play in several, or even many, different positions. Two of Villa's earliest utility players were Willie Groves and Jimmy Crabtree. Though he spent only one season with Villa, Willie Groves played in four different positions. During his career, he occupied nine outfield positions. Jimmy Crabtree, primarily a left-half, played in seven different positions for Villa and in all five defensive positions for his country. Con Martin played in all the defensive positions for Villa during his 213 games for the club, including 27 appearances between the posts, either as stand-in or the club's first choice. Harry Parkes played in all ten outfield positions in a career that spanned 345 first-team games for the club. After the mid-1960s, players were encouraged to become more adaptable and to see their roles as less stereotyped. At the same time, much less attention was paid to the implication of wearing a certain numbered shirt. Accordingly some of the more versatile players came to wear all the different numbered shirts at some stage or another, although this did not necessarily indicate a vast variety of positions. Pat McMahon, Lew Chatterley, Leighton Phillips and Gary Williams all proved their versatility, occupying a good number of different positions during their time with Villa.

V

VAUGHTON, HOWARD. Signed from Wednesbury Strollers in 1880, Howard Vaughton was one of Aston Villa's finest forwards. He was the club's first senior international, capped by England against Ireland in Belfast on 18 February 1882. Vaughton scored five goals on his international debut – England won 13–0 – and went on to appear in five matches for his country. He was also a member of Villa's first FA Cup-winning side which beat West Bromwich Albion in the 1887 final at The Oval. Though his shooting was often classed as erratic, he did score a hat-trick in Villa's 7–4 FA Cup win at Wednesbury Old Athletic in 1883–84. Injury forced his retirement in 1888 and he started a silversmith's business. When the FA Cup was stolen in 1895 after Villa had won it, it was Vaughton's firm who was asked to make a replacement. Vaughton returned to Villa Park as vice-president in 1923, becoming president a year later and in February 1933, he was made a life-member of the club.

VENGLOS, JOZEF. A player for ten years with Czechoslovakian side Slovan Bratislava, Venglos was unable to break into the national side, though he appeared 25 times in the Junior Olympics B team. He retired from playing to complete his studies, becoming a Doctor of Philosophy. After a spell as national manager of Australia, he returned home to manage his former club and took them to two league titles and Cup success. This earned him the position of aide to the national side and in 1976 Czechoslovakia won the European Championship. He took over as national manager in 1978 and in 1980 they were third in the European Championship. He left after a poor World Cup in 1982 but returned for a second spell and took them to the quarter-final stage of the 1990 World Cup. Venglos replaced Graham Taylor as Villa manager in June 1990, but after just one year in office, in which the club finished 17th in the first division, he returned home to his native country.

VICTORIES IN A SEASON – HIGHEST. In the 1971–72 season, Aston Villa won 32 of their 46 league fixtures to win the third division championship, the highest number of wins in a season in the club's history. In 1980–81, they won 26 of their 42 first division matches to win the championship with 60 points, four points ahead of Ipswich Town.

VICTORIES IN A SEASON – LOWEST. Villa's poorest performance in a season was in 1889–90, repeated in 1890–91, when they won just seven matches, though that was out of a 22 match programme. In modern times, their worst record was in seasons 1969–70 and 1986–87 when the club won eight of 42 fixtures. They were relegated on both occasions.

VIDEOS. Aston Villa have produced a number of videos in conjunction with the BBC, the most notable being an official history of the club.

VILLA PARK. The decision to return to the Lower Grounds was taken in January 1896 and much of the credit for the transformation of the amusement park belonged to the club's chairman, Fred Rinder. It was not officially called Villa Park until 1898. The club's first league game, against Blackburn Rovers on 17 April 1897, came just a week after they had equalled Preston's feat of winning the double and a crowd of 15,000 saw Villa win 3–0. Two days later, a near capacity crowd of 35,000 turned up for the visit of Wolves which was combined with a sports meeting. However, despite the club's success on the field, the ground building had left Villa with a huge £10,000 overdraft. This was

Villa Park

paid off by using the ground to stage other games such as an international match between England and Scotland and, in 1901, the first of many FA Cup semi-finals. It was at around this time that Fred Rinder and his assistant architect, Mr E.B. Holmes, made plans to develop Villa Park into a ground capable of holding 120,000. They began by purchasing the seven-acre site for £8,250, along with the offices, carriage drive and bowling green on Trinity Road for an extra £3,500. In the summer of 1914, the cycle track which had encircled the pitch was removed and the banking at both ends of the ground built-up, whilst the Witton Lane Stand was extended. The development of the ground was delayed due to the First World War and it was 1922 when the Trinity Road Stand was built. Though it was first used in August of that year, it was officially opened by the Duke of York (later King George VI) on 26 January 1924 when Villa beat Bolton Wanderers 1–0. The Holte End terracing was extended during the 1930s and was finally completed in 1940, the only ground in the country where development occurred during the hostilities. In March 1946, the biggest crowd to attend a match at Villa Park, 76,588, saw Villa go down 4–3 to Derby County in the first leg of a sixth-round FA Cup tie and even then it was estimated that over

171

6,000 were locked out. Floodlights were installed at the ground in 1958 and were first used when Villa beat Portsmouth 3–2 on 25 August, although they were not officially switched on until the following November for a friendly against Heart of Midlothian. In 1962, the Holte End was covered at a cost of £40,000 and, two years later, the Witton Lane Stand had its unusual roof removed and replaced with a sloping roof. In 1966, Villa Park was chosen as the venue for three World Cup matches which meant that ground improvements were necessary. Villa spent £99,000, £45,000 of which was a government grant, on putting seats in the Witton Lane paddock, covering the players' tunnel with a grill, widening the pitch by three yards, installing 6,250 seats at the Witton Road end of the ground and building a new social club on the bowling green. In February 1977, work began on the £1 million North Stand at the Witton Road end of the ground. The structure itself was superb, but because payments for its completion were badly handled, the police were called in to investigate the club's affairs. They revealed that around £725,000 of work had been unaccounted for. Though Villa won the league championship and European Cup in this period, the club remained deep in debt because of the development of the North Stand. Fans were very bitter about the apparent squandering of money which could quite easily have been spent on strengthening the squad. In 1990, the Holte End's facilities were upgraded and its roof extended at a cost of £450,000. Yet just four years later, it was demolished when it was realised that the ground's conversion into an all-seater stadium could not go ahead with the roof in place. Also that year, the floodlight pylons were removed and new lights mounted along the roofs of all four stands. Other changes included the installation of 2,600 seats on the lower tier of the North Stand and new boxes in the Witton Lane Stand, all of which cost the club £2 million. In 1992, the Trinity Road Stand was completely refurbished at a cost of £2.4 million and in May 1993, work on the Witton Lane Stand began under the expert guidance of stadium manager Ted Small. In May 1994, the Holte End, the largest end terrace in the country, was replaced by the largest end stand in the country at a cost of £5.3 million.

VOWDEN, GEOFF. Jersey-born Geoff Vowden joined Nottingham Forest in the summer of 1958, along with another

Channel Islander, Dick Le Flem. In four years at the City Ground, he scored 40 goals in 90 league games before signing for Birmingham City for £25,000. At St Andrews, he was the club's leading scorer in two seasons and had helped them to the semi-finals of the FA Cup in 1968. He stayed with the Blues until March 1971 when, after having scored 79 goals in 221 League games, he signed for Aston Villa for a fee of £12,500. In his first full campaign with the club, his goals helped Villa win the third division championship but, after suffering a loss of form and a number of niggling injuries, he left competitive football in the winter of 1974 to concentrate on coaching youngsters in the Nottingham area.

W

WAKEMAN, ALAN. A prolific goalscorer as a schoolboy and captain of England Schoolboys, Alan Wakeman started as an office boy at Villa Park and developed his goalkeeping skills with Bloxwich Strollers. In December 1938 he was signed as a professional by Villa and he made his League debut that month in a 2–1 win at Bolton Wanderers, going on to play in six matches that season. During the war, Wakeman guested for a number of clubs and was a regular for Villa in between his job as a Bevin Boy, playing in 191 wartime matches. In 1944 he was an ever-present in the Football League (North) second championship and gained a Cup winners' tankard after Villa had beaten Blackpool 5–4 over two legs. When league football resumed in 1946–47, Wakeman found himself third in line behind Rutherford and Jones and moved to Doncaster Rovers at the end of the 1949–50 season before later playing for Shrewsbury Town.

WALKER, BILLY. Born in Wednesbury in October 1897, the son of George Walker, Billy first played for Hednesford Town and Darlaston and was playing for Wednesbury Old Athletic when Villa signed him on amateur forms in 1915. With Wednesbury Old Athletic, he once scored nine goals in a 40-minute spell and this ability to score goals never left him in the 16 seasons of league football he played for Villa. Making his debut in the FA Cup tie against Queens Park Rangers in 1920, a match in which he scored both goals in a 2–1 victory, he went on to score three more FA Cup goals that season as Villa reached the final at Stamford Bridge, where a goal from Billy Kirton snatched the trophy from Huddersfield Town. Though he was originally a centre-forward, he switched over to the inside-left position, replacing Clem Stephenson towards the end of the following season. He scored 27 goals and won his first England cap against Ireland at Sunderland. All told, Walker won 18 caps for his country. Nicknamed Knocky, Billy Walker was one of the finest players ever to pull on a Villa shirt. He played in 531 league and Cup games and scored 244 goals. He was the first person to score a hat-trick of penalties in a league game, a first division match against Bradford City in November 1927. For 40 years Walker held the Villa record for number of appearances, until overtaken by Charlie Aitken in 1973. Walker's inspirational play helped to make two of Villa's left-wingers into international players; he partnered both Arthur Dorrell and Eric Houghton in the England side. He retired from playing in 1933 and took over as manager of Sheffield Wednesday. He had a short spell in charge at Chelmsford City before becoming manager of Nottingham Forest. At the City Ground, he saw Forest promoted as third division champions in 1950–51 and return to the first division in 1957. He capped his career with victory in the 1959 FA Cup final before illness forced his retirement in 1960.

WALLACE, CHARLIE. Sunderland-born winger Charlie Wallace began his career with the Southwick club before joining Crystal Palace, from whom Villa signed him in 1907. Immediately winning a place in the Villa side, Wallace won two FA Cup winners' and a league championship medals during his nine seasons at Villa Park. During the 1913 FA Cup final at the Crystal Palace, Wallace had the misfortune to miss a penalty in Villa's 1–0 win over Sunderland. His most successful season for the club was 1911–12 when he scored 16 goals in 35 league appearances which led to him winning the first of three international caps for England the following season. Wallace scored 57 goals in 349 league and Cup games for Villa before leaving to join Oldham Athletic in 1921. Two years later, he returned to Villa Park as a club steward, a position he held until 1960.

175

WALSH, DAVE. An Irishman born in Waterford, Dave Walsh was a consistent goalscorer wherever he played. After playing for a number of local clubs, he joined Linfield and in his three years with the club, scored 105 goals, including 60 in the 1945–46 season when the club won the Irish league championship. He joined West Bromwich Albion for £3,500 just prior to the start of the 1946–47 season and scored in each of Albion's first six games. His goals helped the club win promotion to the first division in 1949, but rather surprisingly in December 1950, he was allowed to join Villa, after scoring exactly 100 goals for the Hawthorns club. Though he was not as prolific a scorer at Villa Park, he scored 40 goals in his 114 League and Cup appearances including seven in seven games during the 1953–54 season. An Irish international, winning 29 caps for Northern Ireland and the Republic, six of them whilst with Villa, he joined Walsall for a brief spell before ending his career in non-league football with Worcester City.

WALTERS, JOEY. After making an impressive start to his Villa career, Joey Walters lost form and his place in the side before re-establishing himself in 1908–09. The following season, he scored a hat-trick as Villa beat Manchester United 7–1 on their way to winning the league championship. However, Walters' best season was in 1910–11 when he scored 13 goals in 28 league appearances, including six in successive games, all won by Villa. The Prestwich-born utility forward lost his place towards the end of the 1911–12 season and in the summer moved to Oldham Athletic. He later played for Southend United, Millwall, Manchester United and Rochdale and was actually on the books of his seventh league club when he died of pneumonia, aged 37.

WALTERS, MARK. Villa signed Mark Walters as a 14-year-old associate schoolboy in 1978 following some exciting displays in local schools football. He signed as an apprentice in 1980 and made his league debut coming on as a substitute at home to Leeds United in April 1982, just a few days before he turned professional. Emerging as one of the country's most exciting attacking wingers, he won the first of his nine England Under-21 caps. He continued to thrill Villa supporters for the next few years, scoring some brilliant goals. However, in 1986–87 it all started to go wrong and

Mark Walters

under new manager Billy McNeill, he found himself in and out of the team. Restored to the side when Graham Taylor took charge, he left Villa Park in December 1987 for Glasgow Rangers for £500,000. He had appeared in 225 matches for the Villans, scoring 48 goals. The first black player to play for the Ibrox club, he quickly won over the fans and in his time there won three league championship medals and two Skol League Cup medals. In August 1991, he followed Graeme Souness to Liverpool for £1.25 million after making his England debut against New Zealand on the summer tour of Australasia. He appeared in 124 first-team games for the Anfield club, but after suffering a series of injuries and loan spells at Stoke City and Wolves, he signed for Southampton. Unable to settle at the Dell, he is now playing for Swindon Town.

WARING, TOM. Birkenhead-born Tom 'Pongo' Waring began his professional career with his local club, Tranmere Rovers, in 1926. A couple of years later, he began to show his goalscoring talents when he scored six in Tranmere's 11–1 win over Durham City. It was this kind of form that attracted the League's top clubs and though Arsenal, Bolton and Manchester United had shown an interest in the young Waring, it was Aston Villa who secured his services for £4,700. When he made his debut for Villa in a Central League fixture against rivals Birmingham, a crowd of 23,000 turned out to see him. They were not disappointed as he hit a hat-trick in Villa's victory. When he did play for the first-team against Sunderland at Roker Park, he scored in Villa's 3–2 win. The following season, he hit the first of ten hat-tricks in Villa's colours, as Arsenal were beaten 5–2 at Highbury. In 1930–31, Pongo Waring created a club record by scoring 50 goals, 49 of them in the first division. He scored 13 goals in the first seven games of the season, including all four on the opening day when Villa beat Manchester United 4–3. He also scored four in a 6–1 win over West Ham United and all four in a 4–2 win over Sunderland. In November 1935, after scoring 167 goals in 226 league and Cup matches for Villa, he was surprisingly allowed to join Barnsley. A crowd of over 5,000 showed their disapproval of the move by calling for his return. However, Waring was at Oakwell for less than a year before moving to Wolves and then returning to Tranmere Rovers. He left Prenton Park to play for Accrington

Stanley and later Bath City before ending his playing days guesting for New Brighton during the war.

WARTIME CUP FINAL. The Football League (North) Cup final was played over two legs at the end of the 1943–44 season. Villa lost the first leg at Bloomfield Road 2–1, although according to reports Blackpool looked 'pedestrian and ordinary'. A crowd of 54,824 saw the second leg at Villa Park and they did not have long to wait for Villa to be level on aggregate. Frank Broome headed Villa's opening goal after just 29 seconds following a cross from Iverson. Not to be outdone, Blackpool went straight on the attack and within 90 seconds the scores were level on the day, but the Seasiders led 3–2 on aggregate. Only ten minutes had been played when George Edwards levelled the aggregate score. Five minutes later, Stanley Matthews pounced on a mistake in the Villa six-yard box and Blackpool were 4–3 ahead on aggregate with only a quarter of an hour played. Six minutes before half-time, Bob Iverson cracked home another goal for Villa to make it 4–4 on aggregate. Two minutes into the second half, Broome scored what proved to be the winning goal, Villa taking the Cup 5–4 on aggregate. Charlton Athletic were the Southern League Cup winners and the two clubs met at Stamford Bridge on 20 May 1944. The game ended 1–1 with Eric Houghton scoring Villa's goal.

WARTIME FOOTBALL. *First World War:* In spite of the outbreak of war in 1914, the major football leagues embarked upon their planned programme of matches for the ensuing season and these were completed on schedule at the end of April the following year. Villa finished 13th in the first division and went out of the FA Cup in the second round to Manchester City. The hostilities meant the postponement of Fred Rinder's plans to enlarge Villa Park into a stadium with a capacity of 120,000. The club played little football during the First World War, only entering the Midland Victory League in 1918–19, although they had played West Bromwich Albion over the war years in a series of matches in aid of War Fund.
Second World War: In contrast to the events of 1914, once war was declared on 3 September 1939, the Football League programme of 1939–40 was immediately suspended and the government

forbade any major sporting events, so that for a while there was no football of any description. Villa had opened the season with a 1–1 draw against West Bromwich Albion in a Jubilee match before beating Middlesbrough 2–0 on the opening day of the league season. They then lost 2–1 at home to Everton and 1–0 at Derby County. Villa Park was given over to war use and the Holte End terracing extended, so when Villa played in the Birmingham and District League in 1940–41 and 1941–42, their home games were played on Solihull Town's ground at Shirley. Villa won the Birmingham and District League title in 1941–42 and the following season entered the Football League (North). Also in that season of 1942–43, Villa reached the semi-finals of the Wartime League Cup, where they lost 4–3 to Blackpool over two legs. They gained revenge the following season when they beat the Seasiders 5–4 on aggregate in the final. In 1945–46, Villa participated in the Football League (South) and were beaten to the title by Birmingham City on goal average. Villa scored 106 League goals with George Edwards scoring 39 of them.

WELFORD, JIMMY. Glasgow-born Jimmy Welford moved to the Birmingham area in 1892 to play for Mitchell St George's, from where he signed for Villa the following year. A strong-tackling full-back, he partnered Howard Spencer and with Villa won two league championship medals and an FA Cup winners' medal. He had played in 83 first-team games when in November 1896, he was allowed to join Celtic. With the Parkhead club, Welford won a Scottish league championship medal and Scottish Cup winners' medal before leaving to play in Ireland for Belfast Celtic. In 1900, he won an Irish Cup-winners' medal to become the first player to win English, Scottish and Irish Cup winners' medals, a feat later equalled by Jimmy Delaney.

WELLINGTON ROAD. It was George Ramsay who in 1876 discovered the field at Wellington Road, Perry Barr, sublet by a butcher for just £5 per annum. For the next 21 years it was here that Villa played their home matches and achieved some of their greatest successes. At the junction of Wellington Road and Aston Lane with Birchfield Road stood the Old Crown and Cushion Inn, which was used as the club's headquarters. Match officials changed in a blacksmith's hut that stood opposite the ground. The

Wellington Road ground could hold 27,000, and in January 1888 a then record crowd of 26,849 invaded the pitch twice during the FA Cup tie against Preston North End. The ground also staged two FA Cup semi-finals in 1890 and 1896 and an England v Ireland international game in 1893. By now, Villa's rent had risen to £200 and though the ground had been developed gradually, the club were always on the look-out for new accommodation. The last Villa match to be played at Wellington Road was on Good Friday 1897 when 500 spectators witnessed a reserve-team game against Shrewsbury. Afterwards, the ground was covered by houses. Villa's pavilion was sold to Small Heath and re-erected behind one of the goals at their Muntz Street ground.

WESTON, TOMMY. Left-back Tommy Weston played his early football with Quarry Bank and Old Hill Comrades before joining Coombes Wood in 1909. He joined Villa from Stourbridge in 1911, immediately establishing himself in the club's first team. He played in the Villa side that won the FA Cup in 1913, and in the four seasons leading up to the outbreak of the First World War he developed a great understanding with his full-back colleague Tommy Lyons. After the hostilities, he teamed up with Tommy Smart and appeared in the Villa side that won the FA Cup in 1920. In fact, it was Weston's leg that deflected a goal-bound shot from Huddersfield's Mann to ensure victory. He had played in 179 first-team games for Villa when he joined Stoke in August 1922.

WHELDON, FRED. Known as Diamond, Fred Wheldon was a superb dribbler of the ball, who was capable of beating several players before laying on chances for his team-mates or scoring himself. He joined Villa at the start of their double-winning season, after helping Small Heath to promotion from the second division and though he scored 22 goals in 37 league and Cup appearances, he had an even better season in 1897–98. He scored hat-tricks in each of the first two matches that season and ended the campaign as the club's leading goalscorer with 23 goals in 28 games. He was outstanding in seasons 1898–99 and 1899–1900 as Villa made it three league championship wins in four attempts. Wheldon won four caps for England, scoring a hat-trick on his debut against Ireland in 1897. Against Scotland in 1898, he won a bicycle for scoring the first goal. After netting 74 goals in 138 first-team appearances, Wheldon was transferred to West Bromwich Albion but could not prevent their relegation to the second division. He later played for Queens Park Rangers, Portsmouth and Worcester City before ending his career with Coventry City. An excellent county cricketer, Wheldon scored 4,869 runs for Worcestershire and helped dismiss 93 batsmen as a wicketkeeper.

WHITEHOUSE, JAMES. Goalkeeper James Whitehouse joined Villa from Grimsby Town in the summer of 1896 and took over between the posts from Wilkes. A cool, calm player, Whitehouse was noted for his agility and the speed of his clearances. He played his part in Villa's double-winning season of 1896–97 and had a good game in the FA Cup final win over Everton. He stayed with the club for only two seasons before moving on to a number of other clubs, including Newton Heath and Manchester City.

WILKES, ALBERT. After playing his early football with Oldbury Town, Albert Wilkes joined Walsall where, after impressing against Villa in the Birmingham Charity Cup final, he was offered professional terms. He joined Villa in May 1898 and made his debut in the opening match of the following season, helping the club win the league championship in both 1898–99 and 1899–1900. He won five caps for England, the first against Scotland in 1900–01. Playing mainly at wing-half, he appeared in 157 games for Villa before finishing his career with short spells at Fulham and Chesterfield. Wilkes, who was elected on to Villa's board in 1934, won the Royal Humane Society's award for diving into a West Bromwich park pool to save a young boy.

WILLIAMS, GARY. One of the club's most versatile players, Gary Williams made his Villa debut as a substitute against Everton in September 1978. However, early the following season he was badly injured. After returning to full fitness, he was loaned to Walsall where he helped the Saddlers win promotion to the third division. He returned to Villa Park for the start of the 1980-81 season and ended the campaign with a first division championship medal, later adding European Cup and European Super Cup medals. Chosen to play for the England Under-21 side to face the Republic of Ireland, he was denied his first cap through injury and was not given another chance. He appeared in 302 first-team games for Villa before joining Leeds United in the summer of 1987. He played in 39 league games for the Elland Road club before later playing for Watford and Bradford City.

WILSON ROAD. When Villa played their first match against Aston Brook St Mary's rugby team in March 1875, it was played on a field where Wilson Road, Birchfields now stands. The first half played under Rugby Union code was goalless but in the second half, played under Association rules, Villa scored the only goal of the game. This game was the only competitive fixture to be played by Villa in their initial season of 1874–75 and the only time they played on the ground.

WINS. The club record for the number of league wins over a season is 32 during the 1971–72 season.

WITHE, PETER. Peter Withe played his early football with Southport and Barrow before going to play for Portland Timbers in the USA and Port Elizabeth and Arcadia Shepherds in South Africa. He returned to these shores in November 1973 to play in 17 league games for Wolverhampton Wanderers before joining Birmingham City in 1975. A year later, he signed for Nottingham Forest. Linking well with Tony Woodcock, he headed the club's goalscoring charts in 1976–77 as the club won promotion from the second division. The following season he scored 12 goals, including all four against Ipswich Town as Forest won the league championship. He had a short spell with Newcastle United before joining Villa in May 1980 for a club record fee of £500,000. He had the best years of his career at Villa Park, scoring 20 goals in his first season, as the club won the first division title. It was Withe who scored the only goal of the 1982 European Cup final and during his five seasons with the club, he won 11 England caps. He later played for Sheffield United, Birmingham City (again) and Huddersfield Town, where he was player-coach, before returning to Villa Park as Jozef Venglos's assistant. He later managed Wimbledon but was sacked after just three months and is now back at Villa Park for a third time as the club's chief scout.

WITHERS, COLIN. An England Schoolboy international goalkeeper, Colin Withers made his league debut for

Peter Withe

Birmingham City at White Hart Lane on 19 November 1960 but had a nightmare of a game as Spurs won 6–0. However, he put that performance behind him and went on to play in 116 first-team games for the Blues before Villa signed him for

£18,000 in November 1964. Remarkably, Withers's debut for Villa was also at Tottenham, but this time he only conceded four goals as the Villans went down 4–0. He played in the remaining games that season and in all but four, which were all lost, in 1965–66. He was an ever-present in 1966–67 and in these last two seasons, was the supporters Player of the Year. He appeared in 163 league and Cup games for Villa before being transferred to Lincoln City in the summer of 1969. He played in only one game for the Sincil Bank club before going to Holland to play for Go Ahead Deventer.

WOOSNAM, PHIL. Born in Montgomeryshire, Phil Woosnam appeared for Wales at schoolboy, amateur and youth levels before playing for Manchester City as an amateur. During his four years at Maine Road, he was studying at Bangor University and appeared in only one league game for the club. After National Service, he joined Leyton Orient and in four seasons with the Brisbane Road club, scored 19 goals in 108 league games. In November 1958 he joined West Ham United for £30,000 and in yet another four-year spell with a club, scored 26 goals in 138 league appearances. By now, Woosnam was a full Welsh international and when he signed for Villa in November 1962 for £27,000 he had already won 15 caps. An instant success with the Villa Park faithful, he made his debut at home to Bolton Wanderers, having a hand in all but one of Villa's goals in a 5-0 win. Though never a prolific scorer, he scored 20 goals in 40 league and Cup appearances in 1965–66 before surprisingly leaving the club in the close season to become manager-coach of the Atlanta Chiefs. In 1969, he was appointed Commissioner of the NASL and the following year he coached the USA World Cup side.

WORLD CLUB CHAMPIONSHIP. Villa faced Penarol of Uruguay in the World Club Championship in Tokyo on 12 December 1982, but went down 2–0.

WORLD CUP. In 1966, three World Cup matches were staged at Villa Park:

13 July	Argentina 2 Spain 1	42,738
16 July	Argentina 0 West Germany 0	46,587
20 July	Spain 1 West Germany 2	45,187

Alan Wright

WORST START. The club's worst-ever start to a season was in 1969-70. It took ten league games to record the first victory of the season, drawing just two and losing seven of the opening fixtures. The run ended with a 3–2 success over Hull City at Villa Park on 20 September 1969. The club then lost just one of their next seven games but were still relegated to the third division for the first time in their history.

WRIGHT, ALAN. The youngest player to play for Blackpool, Alan Wright made his League debut for the Seasiders as a substitute against Chesterfield on 2 May 1988 at the age of 16 years and 217 days. Over the next couple of seasons, he played in a variety of positions before settling at left-back, where he appeared in all but the first game of the 1990-91 season. He had made 57 consecutive league appearances for the Bloomfield Road club when he became Kenny Dalglish's first signing for Blackburn Rovers in October 1991. An important member of the side that won promotion to the first division via the play-offs, he missed few games until problems with his stomach muscles led to an operation. In March 1995 after playing in 88 league and Cup games for the Ewood

186

Park club, he joined Aston Villa in a £1 million deal. He made his debut at West Ham United and was an ever-present in 1995–96 when he won his first medal, Villa beating Leeds United in the League Cup final. He also won a call up to the full England squad.

WRIGHT, MICK. Born at Ellesmere Port, Cheshire, Mick Wright made his league debut for Villa at Blackpool in September 1963 in a 4–0 win, just days before he turned professional. In 1964, he played for England youth and followed that up with Under-18 caps the following year. Full-back Wright spent ten years at Villa Park, playing in 315 league and Cup games before injury forced him to retire in May 1973. He won a third division championship medal in 1972, which in some part made up for him missing Villa's appearance in the 1971 League Cup final.

WYLIE, RON. Ron Wylie made his league debut for Notts County in 1951, joining Villa some seven years later for £9,250 after scoring 33 goals in 227 league games for the Meadow Lane club. Wylie soon settled into the Villa side and wearing the Number 10 shirt formed a fine left-wing partnership with Irishman Peter McParland. The pair helped Villa to promotion in 1959–60 and to the League Cup in 1961. During the early '60s, Wylie was club captain but after playing in 245 first-team games in which he scored 27 goals, he left Villa Park for rivals Birmingham City. At St Andrews, he appeared in 128 League games before returning to Villa Park as coach in the summer of 1970. He moved on to Coventry City, first as coach and later as assistant manager, before going to work in Cyprus and Hong Kong. In July 1982, he returned to England to manage West Bromwich Albion but in 1984 he returned to Villa Park for a third time as coach to the second team. He lost his job when Graham Taylor was appointed manager but returned to the club for a fourth time in 1990 as Villa's Community Liaison Officer.

X

X. In football X traditionally stands for a draw. The club record for the number of draws in a season is 17. In 1975–76 they managed 17 draws out of 42 matches.

XMAS DAY. There was a time when football matches were regularly played on Christmas Day, but in recent years the game's authorities have dropped the fixture from the calendar. The last time Villa played on Christmas Day was in 1956 when they went down 1–0 to Sunderland at Roker Park. There have been a number of memorable games played on Christmas Day, including a 4–0 win over Nottingham Forest in 1907 when Joe Bache scored all four goals. In the first two seasons after the First World War, Villa beat Chelsea 5–2 in 1919 and went down 4–0 at home to Manchester United the year after. In 1931, Villa beat Middlesbrough 7–1 with both Houghton and Beresford grabbing hat-tricks. There have also been some exciting encounters with Wolverhampton Wanderers. In 1933, Villa won 6–2, though Wolves gained revenge in 1948 with a 4–0 win at Molineux. The two clubs last met on Christmas Day in 1951 when Walsh, Dixon and Goffin scored for Villa in a 3–3 draw.

Y

YORK, DICKY. Born in Handsworth, Dicky York ran for Birchfield Harriers when he was only eight years old and when Villa won the FA Cup in 1913, York represented England Boys. While at grammar school, he preferred rugby to soccer and was an outstanding outside-half. During the latter stages of the First World War, York, who served with the Royal Flying Corps, guested for Chelsea but in May 1919 he signed for Villa, making his debut in the 2–1 defeat at Sunderland on the opening day of the 1919–20 season. His early outings for the club were at right-half behind Charlie Wallace, the player he eventually replaced in Villa's attack. A fast, direct winger, he made two appearances for England

Dicky York

and played for Villa in the 1924 FA Cup final. He scored two hat-tricks for Villa, both against Bury (away 3–2 1925–26 and home 7–1 1928–29) but after 390 first-team games in which he scored 86 goals, he joined Port Vale. After a season at Vale Park, he moved on to Brierley Hill Alliance, retiring two years later.

YORKE, DWIGHT. A versatile forward who is capable of playing on either flank or up front as an out and out striker, Dwight Yorke created such a good impression when playing for Trinidad and Tobago against Aston Villa that Graham Taylor moved in quickly to sign him from his club, Signal Hill, for £120,000. After a short period of acclimatisation at Villa Park, Yorke made his league debut as a substitute at Selhurst Park. Villa lost 1–0 to Crystal Palace. He appeared in 18 League games in 1990–91 when Jozef Venglos was manager but the following season when Ron Atkinson

Dwight Yorke

had assumed control, he had an outstanding campaign. He top scored with 11 goals in the league plus another five in Cup matches, including a first-half hat-trick at Derby County in a fifth-round FA Cup match. He had a more unpredictable campaign in 1992–93, scoring only seven goals. Some of them were memorable, including a superb diving header in the 2–0 win over Ipswich Town. In 1993–94 he spent most of the time on the substitutes bench, though in the last game of the season at home to Liverpool, he came on for Beinlich and scored both Villa goals in a 2–1 win. In 1994–95 he made only one appearance for Trinidad and Tobago after receiving permission to miss the Pan American Tournament in March 1995 because he did not want to endanger his place with Villa. In 1995–96, Yorke had his best season to date when he scored 25 league and Cup goals, including one in the League Cup final victory over Leeds United. When Villa played the Elland Road club on 3 February 1996, Yorke notched his 50th goal in all competitions. He also established the Premier League record for the competition's fastest goal when he scored after just 13 seconds in the 3–0 win over Coventry City. If it had not been for his previous qualification for Trinidad and Tobago, he would undoubtedly have worn an England shirt.

YOUNGEST PLAYER. The youngest player to appear in a first-class fixture for Aston Villa is Jimmy Brown who played in the second division match against Bolton Wanderers (away 1–2) on 17 September 1969 when he was 15 years and 349 days old.

YOUTH CUP. Aston Villa have appeared in the FA Youth Cup final on three occasions. With the exception of the 1978 final, they were two-legged affairs. The aggregate scores are:
1972   Aston Villa 5 Liverpool 2
1978   Crystal Palace 1 Aston Villa 0 (one game only)
1980   Aston Villa 3 Manchester City 2

Z

ZENITH. Few fans will argue over which moment has been the finest in the club's history. In 1896–97, Aston Villa became only the second club at that time to achieve the double – winning the league championship and FA Cup in the same season. They won the first division by a clear 11 points and beat Everton 3–2 in the cup final.

ZENITH DATA SYSTEMS CUP. The Zenith Data Systems Cup replaced the Simod Cup from the 1989–90 season for three seasons. Villa defeated Hull City at Boothferry Park 2–1, Nottingham Forest by the same score at Villa Park and Leeds United 2–0 also at Villa Park to reach the area final. David Platt scored in each of those three matches with two of his goals coming from the penalty spot. Facing Middlesbrough, Villa lost the first leg of the area final at Ayresome Park 2–1 and then lost by the same score at home after extra time thus missing the chance of going to Wembley. The club did not enter the competition the following season but in 1991–92, beat Coventry City 2–0 at Highfield Road before going out to Nottingham Forest by the same scoreline, in what proved to be their last game in the competition.